THE
TRAVELER'S
EYE

THE TRAVELER'S EYE

A Guide to Still and Video Travel Photography

Lisl Dennis

CLARKSON POTTER/PUBLISHERS

NEW YORK

The Buddha's eyes painted on the Swayambunath Stupa in Kathmandu, Nepal, are a much photographed symbol of spiritual mystery; I composed a tight vertical image of one eye with an 80–200mm zoom lens. *(jacket)*

In Thailand at Wat Po, I used an 80–200mm lens to zero in on the Buddha's curly gold hair. *(page 1)*

The Zia sun symbol painted on an adobe wall in Santa Fe became a surreal shot by composing up-close with a 28mm lens. *(page 2)*

I used a 60mm macro lens for a close-up of the knot on a Thai monk's saffron robe. *(page 5)*

This shot of the patterned light in an outdoor café in Rabat, Morocco, called for average metering. *(pages 6–7)*

On a Nepalese trek, I personalized my walking stick with a farmer's handkerchief and yak jewelry—The dyed-hair earrings and tail ornaments used to distinquish one herd from another. Waking one morning at seventeen thousand feet to a stunning sight of the Himalayas, I staggered off to take a picture of my staff against a rock. *(page 9)*

In Santa Fe, Native Americans sell jewelry under the portal of the Palace of the Governors. I zeroed in on this woman's hands surrounded by the swirl of color in her dress. *(pages 10–11)*

Copyright © 1996 by Lisl Dennis

All rights reserved. No part of this book may be reproduced or transmitted in any form or by any means, electronic or mechanical, including photocopying, recording, or by any information storage and retrieval system, without permission in writing from the publisher.

Published by Clarkson N. Potter, Inc., a division of Crown Publishers, Inc., 201 East 50th Street, New York, New York 10022. Member of the Crown Publishing Group.

Random House, Inc. New York, Toronto, London, Sydney, Auckland

Potter Books and colophon are trademarks of Crown Publishers, Inc.

Manufactured in China

Design by Margaret Hinders

Library of Congress Cataloging-in-Publication Data

Dennis, Lisl.
    The traveler's eye / by Lisl Dennis.
       p.   cm.
    Includes bibliographical references and index.
    1. Travel photography. I. Title.
    TR790.D466 1996   95-23733
    778.9'991–dc20   CIP

ISBN 0-517-70573-7

10 9 8 7 6 5 4 3 2 1

First Edition

CONTENTS

ACKNOWLEDGMENTS

A book such as *The Traveler's Eye* has a long gestation period—practically a lifetime. So to begin with the basics, I am increasingly appreciative of my parents, Elizabeth Macy Jones and James Suydam Jones. They encouraged me to look around from day one and fostered a high level of visual culture throughout my childhood and adolescence. To my uncle, William Davis Taylor, former publisher of the *Boston Globe,* I owe a debt of gratitude for kicking off my photography career on the staff of the newspaper. I am grateful to my husband, Landt Dennis, who has supported my creativity as a travel photographer and patiently waited around for a quarter of a century while I've taken thousands of photographs all over the world. My agent, Helen F. Pratt, is the best support an obsessive, creative person could possibly hope to have. And to Lauren Shakely, Annetta Hanna, Pam Krauss, Roy Finamore, Howard Klein, and Maggie Hinders—practically the entire staff at Potter—with whom I have worked on this and other books, I am grateful for the privilege of having *The Traveler's Eye* published by a company with the highest standards in the industry.

The least you can do is be there.

ANNIE DILLARD
Pilgrim at Tinker Creek

To Terri —
Thanks for being there!
Jill Denny

INTRODUCTION

· ·

Santa Fe, New Mexico, is where this book was born. In 1980 my husband, Landt Dennis, and I founded the Travel Photography Workshop in Santa Fe. The Traveler's Eye contains the essence of the curriculum that I have developed over my nearly thirty years of far-flung personal travels and foreign assignments for magazines, books, and commercial clients. More important, the curriculum of the Travel Photography Workshop in Santa Fe is based on what I've learned through many years of teaching and leading photography tours all over the world. The queries and demands of hundreds of participants have made me acutely aware of the creative aspirations and personal concerns of serious amateur and aspiring professional travel photographers. While unable to duplicate the spontaneous spirit and personal interaction of the workshop experience, I cover the curriculum here in *The Traveler's Eye*, and in fact, the book format lends itself to a more thorough treatment of certain topics.

I am frequently asked how the workshop began and why Santa Fe? Many years ago, I was asked by a publisher to produce my first book on travel photography. The editor knew my work from the early portfolio spreads I was getting in travel and photography magazines. As a result of these book and magazine articles, I began receiving letters and telephone calls from readers asking me to critique their work and to give them advice on various aspects of travel photography. Eventually, I lacked the time to adequately respond to these inquiries. As letters lay unanswered and calls went unreturned, I realized the great interest in this area.

CONSTRUCTION AND RESTORATION of national monuments is an ongoing problem for the travel photographer. Expecting to take traditional shots of Bangkok's temple complexes, I was faced with scaffolding, debris, and Buddhas wrapped in saffron swaddling clothes to protect them from the dust. Disappointed, I took a while to recognize the marvel of what was going on. The temples were under restoration in honor of the two hundredth anniversary of the reigning Chakri dynasty. I had a once-in-a-lifetime photojournalistic opportunity before me. Changing my attitude about what constituted viable travel photography, I spent several days temple hopping in pursuit of the series of images shown in this chapter that reflect the reality of Bangkok at the time.

Spreading out a map of the United States on the living-room floor of our New York City apartment, Landt and I scanned America for a location in which to found a workshop. After considering several spots from coast to coast, we chose Santa Fe, New Mexico. From New York City we organized the first Travel Photography Workshop in Santa Fe. Much to our delight, participants came from all over the country. The first year we discovered that Santa Fe was perfect from every point of view: it is the most foreign destination in the United States, with the city and its surroundings the home of Hispanic, Native American, and Anglo cultures. Centuries-old Spanish-colonial churches and Indian pueblos exist in a natural environment of spectacular landscapes and kaleidoscopic skies. Miraculously, local traditions still stand up despite the increasing development of New Mexico.

My workshops in Santa Fe have thrived, I believe, because increasing global

tourism and worldwide social, economic, and political changes have altered the ground rules for destination photographers. It used to be that all you had to do was point your camera and stop the action on the picturesque, the quaint, the authentic, the exotic. The world now presents new challenges that, indeed, more than meet the eye. No longer does the world sit pretty and say "cheese" for photographers, whether they be amateurs or professionals. Good destination photographs are no longer free, part of the package price of the trip; they must be worked for and earned.

The biggest challenge today's travel photographer faces is the ever-widening gap between the mythological travel photograph and the reality of destinations today. Postcards feature fossilized images of Notre Dame, the Coliseum, the Tower of London. They don't show the parking lots, souvenir stands, and crowds that now surround these monuments. The picture of Venice's San Marco cathedral in a tour brochure doesn't reveal the scaffolding tourists saw it wearing for over a decade. The street scenes in a travel book on Greece are miraculously free of the telephone wires and craft-shop signs that are ubiquitous today.

Illustrations in a travel magazine for an African safari look as if Ralph

Lauren and Isak Dinesen styled them, with not one shot of a lion surrounded by thirty vans sprouting tourists and telephotos—a common contemporary safari experience. An ad for Garuda Airlines casts Balinese harvesting the terraced rice fields while wearing ethnic sarongs and colorful conical straw hats tinted by a computer. Lured to Bali by this Madison Avenue image, you'll find, as I did, that the harvesters today are wearing Western running shorts and baseball caps—who wants to slog around in a rice field in a sarong, anyway?

Due to pollution and the impact of tourists, the Parthenon has been structurally compromised; you can no longer walk through the monument and angle up on the splendid columns; neither can you lose yourself within Stonehenge. Due to bomb threats, visitors are often restricted from walking on the terrace around the Taj Mahal. A high-rise apartment building has sprung up underneath the Eiffel Tower, compromising the traditional straight-on shot of the structure from the Trocadéro. But, mark my words, we'll continue to see promotional travel photographs that present these places from angles no longer possible.

Professional travel photography has been and continues to be a vehicle for promoting tourism. But it's increasingly difficult to derive a true sense of what you will experience at a destination by looking at promotional tourist material and articles in travel magazines. Nor can you judge whether a particular place is going to provide good travel photographs just by looking at published photographs—what you see is not what you get.

But should the world remain the same? In writing about his travels through the Far East, Pico Iyer says in *Video Night in Kathmandu,* "A kind of imperial arrogance underlies the very assumption that the people of the developing world should be happier without the TVs and motorbikes that we find so indispensable in ours. If money does not buy happiness, neither does poverty."

The homogenization of the global village is a big issue for image makers restricted by straight, unmanipulated photography. Painters can do a watercolor of a Caribbean market and eliminate contemporary distractions from the old-world charm of the scene. The travel photographer cannot edit the environment to such an extent. Although you can change your angle or resort to computer retouching, these tactics aren't always enough to offset reality.

So what can you do? First, you can change your reactions to a changing world. You can redefine what travel photography is. Moreover, you can rethink what constitutes a viable travel image in the last decade of the twentieth century. You can blow the lid off preconceived ideas of what you will be photographing in a particular destination.

Like me, you might not celebrate all the inescapable changes, but you can refuse to be shut down photographically by them. After all, the symbols of the twentieth century are all around us at home and abroad; they are contemporary realities. As such they are viable subjects for the traveler's camera; they are part of the travel experience. I do not suggest you focus on these symbols as ugly elements in order to make a deliberately negative statement about the travel experience. But today's world can come together in fascinating, amusing, and graphically effective photographs if you're willing to open up your thinking to contemporary situations as fresh raw material for destination images.

The Traveler's Eye is written for travel photographers who not only want to

sharpen their technical skills but also wish to enhance the visual impact in their destination imagery. You may be a bit bored with the pictures you've taken in the past; you may want to expand your personal definition of travel photography. In this book we won't ignore how to take better traditional travel pictures. But, I will encourage you to consider unorthodox aesthetic treatments of traditional travel themes.

The illustrations in *The Traveler's Eye* were shot worldwide. However, the ideas I share and the techniques I discuss are equally applicable at home. Further, they are not dependent on the latest "I can think for you" equipment. The essence of my teaching falls into two categories: personal opinion evolved from my own travel experiences and universal creative principles. These ideas can be applied to any subject matter anywhere in the world with just about any equipment.

The Traveler's Eye is not as formulaic as many other how-to photography books, although I certainly honor the rules wherever applicable or unavoidable. My goal is to help the destination photographer, whether experienced or a novice, translate experience and feeling onto film. This cannot be done by venturing out into the world with programmed ideas of what is to be recorded and

how to respond to subjects personally and creatively.

Kodak estimates that more than 75 percent of all still photographs taken in the world are travel and vacation related. While the sophisticated autofocus SLR camera remains the medium popular with those dedicated to the art and craft of the still travel image, the video camera now replaces the "point and shoot" still camera in the hands of many travelers. For this reason, *The Traveler's Eye* also addresses the interests of the travel-video shooter. This section guides the student in conceptualizing and constructing effective vacation video shows. After all, the personal and creative challenges of a foreign environment are no less significant for the person wielding a video camera rather than an SLR camera.

Along with video, I continue to devote myself to straightforward destination photography because I constantly discover new things as I immerse myself in foreign environments with my camera. I'm convinced that travel photography remains a personal frontier for style; many unique visual symbols, old and new, captured on film, can reflect my evolving relationship to the world. The images in this book represent my personal photographic past life. I hope that reading the book will inform and enrich your future photographic life.

THE ORIGINS OF TRAVEL PHOTOGRAPHY

....

My FIRST NAIVE ATTEMPTS TO take travel photographs remain indelibly exposed in my consciousness. Living and traveling in Europe right after high school, I aimed my camera at the spring crocuses growing at King's College, Cambridge, at the characters posing in front of Irish pubs, at the snowscapes around Swiss ski resorts, and at Sicily's smoking Mt. Etna. These images—long faded from celluloid—are distinct memories from my earliest photographic explorations of the world.

Give or take a stop, the proper exposure of my photographic memories brings to light the many lessons I've learned as a lover of travel photography. It is these experiences I wish to share in *The Traveler's Eye*. Before embarking on the odyssey of improving our destination photographs, however, it's important to know the origins of the medium and to understand the imperatives—the underlying irresistible reasons—that have made photography and the travel experience so closely intertwined, yesterday and today.

From a single impression on a wet glass plate to the hundreds of images spinning on an interactive CD-ROM, travel photography has a grand heritage, one that coincides closely with the history of the medium. The invention of photography is attributed to Nicephore Niepce and Louis-Jacques-Mandé Daguerre, two Frenchmen who first competed and later collaborated in the development of the daguerreotype. Their process of affixing an image on the silvered surface of a copper plate was unveiled in Paris in 1839. Unknown to Niepce and Daguerre, William Henry Fox Talbot was working in England at the same time to perfect a photographic process called the calotype or talbotype. Talbot's experience is of special significance to the origins of travel photography. On a trip to the Italian Lake District in 1833, Talbot became frustrated with his inability to make respectable pencil sketches with the *camera lucida*, an early instrument that aided artists in rendering a scene accurately.

THE DECORATIVE NATURE of Egyptian hieroglyphics and modern script attracted my eye throughout Egypt, arguably the world's most historic destination for travel photography. I was framing the door of a truck with a 28mm lens for a portrait when the driver unexpectedly held a chicken aloft, its wing gracefully echoing the script below. I shot quickly to take advantage of Egyptian serendipity. *(page 20)* While photogenic hieroglyphics were ubiquitous on all the temples, I preferred the more unexpected, including the colorful script found on chair covers and on many produce bags in marketplaces. *(preceding page and above)*

Talbot's recounting of the experience can be read in Beaumont Newhall's *The History of Photography:* "I was amusing myself on the lovely shores of the Lake of Como in Italy, taking sketches with Wollaston's camera lucida. . . . After various fruitless attempts I laid aside the instrument and came to the conclusion that its use required a previous knowledge of drawing which, unfortunately, I did not possess. I then thought of trying again a method which I had tried many years before. This method was to take a *camera obscure* and to throw the image of the objects on a piece of paper in its focus. . . . It was during these thoughts that the idea occurred to me—how charming it would be if it were possible to cause these natural images to imprint themselves durably, and remain fixed upon the paper."

Talbot, who invented the first negative-positive technique, went on to publish the hallmark series of volumes titled *The Pencil of Nature* in 1844. Its architectural studies, still lifes, and scenes of daily life around Lacock Abbey in England can be seen today in a museum dedicated to Talbot's discoveries.

Inscribed on the title page of *The Pencil of Nature* is a Latin verse from Virgil's *Georgics:* "It is a joyous thing to be the first to cross a mountain." Indeed, armed with their camera obscuras, increasing numbers of adventurous amateur photographers began crossing the mountains and valleys of the world in pursuit of travel imagery, generally referred to by photography historians as "exploratory" or "topographical" photography.

IN A LUXOR MARKET, three Egyptian women buying fabic presented an exposure dilemma. I knew I would need to compensate for the black volumes of the women's robes. Calculating that the black occupied more than two-thirds of the image area, I selected minus one stop on my exposure-compensation dial. Then I autobracketed the exposure one stop to ensure a proper exposure on slide film. When calculating exposure compensation, remember: too dark, less light; too bright, more light.

Thus, the customary and cultivated practice of traveling with a sketch pad and diary began to decline. A mere decade after his Lake Como experience, Talbot wrote, "Already sundry amateurs have laid down the pencil and armed themselves with chemical solutions and with *camera obscure.* These amateurs especially, and they are not a few, who find the rules of perspective difficult to learn and to apply—and who, moreover, have the misfortune to be lazy—prefer to use a method which dispenses with all trouble."

On my own Italian sojourn at the age of eighteen, I too had "the misfortune to be lazy" and found "the rules of perspective difficult to learn and to apply." From early childhood I wanted to become an artist of some sort. To this end I was ostensibly trying my hand at sculpture at the Accademia dei Belli Arti in Florence. I soon found the confines of a studio physically stifling and the strict discipline of classical, European art training too rigorous. Playing hooky from sculpture class, I frequently hopped an early-morning bus and headed for the Tuscan countryside with a picnic and a camera. Passing by farmhouses along the way, I established rapport with the country people. With my fractured Italian and my first camera, I came away with portraits that seemed to be far easier to pull off than the clay bust I was messing with back in the studio.

In Italy the multifaceted social and creative connections engendered by the camera soon had me hooked on photography. I had become another amateur in pursuit of "photo-souvenirs," as they were called in the nineteenth century; I went on to learn about the history of travel photography.

EGYPT IS REPLETE with photo opportunities that invoke the early images of such nineteenth-century explorer/photographers as Felix Teynard, Francis Frith, Maxime Du Camp, and Felix Beato. Not much has changed since these Europeans ventured into the Valley of the Kings and Queens or the Temple of Luxor with their large-format, wet-plate camera systems loaded onto donkeys and camels. The mysterious, ever-moving light penetrating temples and wrapping around carved columns remains.

During the decades immediately following the invention of photography, European amateurs exported it around the globe. By the middle of the nineteenth century, travelers who were not photographers in their own right began purchasing photo-souvenirs, and to meet the growing demand for these, enterprising amateurs quickly turned professional. Among the best of those who set up shop catering to wealthy European visitors was a former bank clerk from Nottingham, England, Samuel Bourne, who, with Charles Sheperd, did a brisk business creating "aide-memoire" prints from Simla, India.

Taking advantage of the same growing market was Francis Frith. In 1860, he established Frith & Co. in England, which soon became the largest European producer of photographs of the Middle East, the British Isles, and the Continent. Using the more sophisticated wet-plate collodion process developed in the 1850s, Frith made a big hit with the publication of *Egypt and Palestine Photographed and Described*. It was an ambitious set of books, with images printed and tipped into the volumes by hand. *The British Journal of Photography*'s review of these volumes makes them sound like a harbinger of the coffee-table book, noting that they were "got up in a style that renders them fit ornament for any drawing room."

With the Grand Tour in full swing by the 1860s, some travelers eschewed locally produced commercial prints. For example, the Prince of Wales hired Frances Bedford as his official staff photographer for an 1862 Grand Tour to the Holy Land, Egypt, Constantinople, and the Mediterranean, while the Bisson Frères, brothers Louis-Auguste and Auguste-Rosalie, accompanied Napoleon III and the Empress Eugénie to Switzerland in 1860 to produce an aide-memoire album titled *Le Mont Blanc et ses Glaciers; Souvenirs du Voyage de L.L. Majestés l'Empereur et l'Impératrice.*

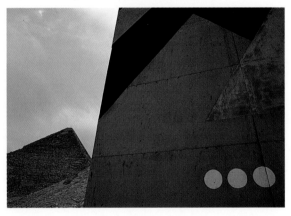

Travel photography and commercial interests were wed from the very outset of the medium. Deborah Bull and Donald Lorimer, authors of *Up the Nile: A Photographic Excursion, Egypt 1839–1898,* note that early photography was taken up with the same pioneering spirit as the geographic exploration of the era, impelled by a genuine sense of scientific and cultural inquiry. Fueled by the public's desire to purchase novel images of exotic places, photography in turn directly stimulated tourism, expanding the borders of the Grand Tour beyond Italy and Greece, beyond the Mediterranean basin to the Near East, the Orient, and eventually to the American West. As Bull and Lorimer write, "The pictures appealed to a public that had responded . . . not only by buying them, but by traveling in increasing numbers to the Middle East to see the land for themselves."

WHEN I VISITED the pyramids at Giza, incursions of modernity included tour groups, souvenir stands, commercial camel rides, and a huge billboard promoting a sound-and-light show. Another problem that day was the dust-stormy sky. As I approached the pyramids, a billboard caught my attention. Playing around with a 24mm lens, I saw the relationships of color and the repeating pyramidal shapes. Modern symbols often work their way into my destination images. Whenever possible, I try to join these contemporary elements rather than fight them.

By the end of the nineteenth century, the market for travel prints by professional photographers in faraway places had begun to fall off. The invention of roll film made it possible for tourists to take their own shots, using handheld cameras that replaced the unwieldy equipment of earlier days. "You press the button, we do the rest," was George Eastman's promotional slogan for his nifty new box camera, the Kodak, which came out in 1888. With the introduction of the Kodak, travelers were finally photographically self-sufficient, and travel photography was now squarely in the hands of the amateur shooter, where it remains to this day.

Throughout the twentieth century, however, a handful of professionals have further popularized travel photography. Of notable interest was Wallace Nutting, a Congregational minister, author, publisher, and collector of antiques. Around the turn of the century, Nutting was bitten by the travel-photography bug. He left his home in Framingham, Massachusetts, to photograph the United States and Canada, as well as thirteen countries abroad. Wallace Nutting is believed to have printed and sold more photographs by a single individual than anyone else in the entire history of the medium, both directly and through the mail. The romantic pictorialism in his series of books—*England Beautiful, Ireland Beautiful, Maine Beautiful,* and *Virginia Beautiful,* to name a few titles—are part of the early heritage of published color travel photography.

Later, during the 1920s and 1930s, Burton Holmes became the rage on the American travel lecture circuit. Dressed in white tie and tails, Holmes drew capacity crowds at camera clubs and town halls with his travel films and slide lectures. Interestingly, Holmes was the first professional of any significance to actually call himself a "travel photographer."

The popularity of Burton Holmes's slide lectures had faded by World War II. Not long after that, however, came the birth of travel photography magazines with *Holiday, Venture,* and *Travel & Camera* emerging as forums for travel photography at its finest during the late fifties, sixties, and early seventies. Today, magazines such as *Travel & Leisure, Conde Nast Traveler, Travel Holiday,* and *National Geographic Traveler* feature the work of professionals who are more apt to be photojournalists or fashion or interior-design photographers than travel specialists per se. One reason for the broad spectrum of contributors is that, compared to other commercial applications of the medium, travel photography is far from being a lucrative field for the professional. Few professionals today can afford to specialize in the travel industry. Nevertheless, studio-bound pros jump to accept the occasional travel assignment to a far-flung place, eager for a photographic experience outside the controlled routine of their commercial work. Editorial travel assignments may, in fact, give commercial professionals a taste once again of what it's like to be an amateur shooter on vacation.

For both amateurs and professionals, destination photography remains a frontier for style and personal exploration. What I find exciting and challenging about the work is the opportunity to build on my past images and personal experience. I know that my future destination photographs will be taken more with the mind's eye than with the optic nerve. As I become willing to probe more personal photographic frontiers, the *process* of travel photography becomes more and more important to me, rather than the resulting images.

AFTER A HOT, DUSTY DAY of digging for pharaonic treasures, archaeologist Howard Carter, who excavated Tutankhamen's tomb in 1922, probably sat in a chair like these and kicked back with a gin and tonic. Shot with an 80–200mm zoom lens from my room at the Winter Palace in Luxor, the image evokes a twenties atmosphere. I respond to any travel-photo opportunity that captures the remnants of a *temps perdu*.

What are these personal frontiers? Ranier Fabian and Hans-Christian Adam give the answer in the closing words of *Masters of Early Travel Photography:* "Those now eager to undertake journeys of discovery must do it through their own minds, since no wilderness or virgin territory remains to be discovered. But some intellects are as vast as a continent, as undiscovered as the Old West once was, as full of surprises as the classic East. There is a whole new generation whose members have grown up aware that the only trip available to them, or worth making, leads into their own heads."

And, I would add . . . hearts!

Susan Sontag corroborates this in *On Photography* when she writes, "The camera makes everyone a tourist in other people's realities–and eventually in one's own."

I DIDN'T CHANNEL King Tut to create this
unusual composition at Abu Simbel of a guard
holding an ankh, a sacred symbol of eternal
life. Many of my unorthodox destination photographs are based on mere observation of
what is going on in the environment. The guard
was actually holding the ankh behind his back.
Being more interested in the shape and symbol-
ism of the ankh than in a conventional portrait
of him holding the thing up, I went with my initial instinct to photograph the man from the
back, with the temple beyond. *(above)*

DISTORTION IS THE principal optical quality
of wide-angle lenses. Rather than attempting to
avoid or control distortion, I often use it to dra-
matize a foreground element. At the Temple of
Philae, I moved in close with a 20mm lens to
exaggerate the volume of the stone carving and
to create greater dimensionality between the
foreground and background. I also use this
technique to eliminate unwanted elements,
such as garbage or a parked car, from a composition. I simply cover the intrusion by dropping
it behind a strong, distorted foreground.
(opposite)

THE TRAVEL STILL LIFE has always appealed to me as a way to interpret certain aspects of the destination experience. My husband, Landt, was ordering some djellabas in a Luxor market when the Egyptian cotton rolled from the bolts onto the shop floor. I simply aimed down and concentrated on the striped fabric in a still-life composition. *(above)*

AN EGYPTIAN STAKEOUT resulted in an amusing shot of a passerby gazing at a tableau awaiting installation on the sidewalk. Positioning myself on the opposite sidewalk with my camera on a tripod, I waited for the right person to enter the frame. The motion in his swinging djellaba did not bother me in this instance. However, to completely stop motion in elements moving laterally across the film plane, use a 250th of a second shutter speed. This will stop passersby dead in their tracks. *(right)*

CREATIVITY AND THE TRAVELING EYE

···

THE EYE HAS TO TRAVEL," DECLARED
the late Diana Vreeland. The longtime editor of *Harper's Bazaar* and *Vogue*
magazines, Vreeland sponsored extravagant fashion shoots in third-world
countries in the 1950s, with glamorous models steeped in exotica and surrounded by ethnicity. Why did she feel that such photographs of foreignness
would sell haute couture?

Vreeland must have realized that the lure of the travel venue—even if limited to the pages of a magazine—would allow readers to make a double

projection. They could not only project themselves into the dress but also into a whole new persona unfettered by the familiar and the conventional. She was saying, "Go for it! Put on a dramatic Balenciaga evening dress; throw yourself into a challenging culture, try out a new exotic sense of self; be different!" Isn't this what we all hope to experience when we travel?

Filled with the desire for fresh awareness, we proclaim to friends or family, "Let's go!" Loosing ourselves from the moorings of daily life, we embark on the creative process of travel, projecting ourselves into the sights, sounds, and smells of a foreign life. We might be better off there than here: we might feel better, look better, eat better, love better, see better . . . be more creative. For many amateur travel photographers, the lure of the exotic is, indeed, key to the creative process. But for those, like me, who take on travel photography as a serious medium for artistic expression, it's necessary to make the creative process quite conscious and to recognize the specific challenges of the field.

CULTURAL DISORIENTATION often blocks our photographic response to unfamiliar and curious sights. Having no personal, intellectual, and cultural frame of reference for the peculiar photo opportunity, we tune it out. To counter this, I try to allow myself to be visually seduced by the otherness of these symbols. For instance, in front of the Oriental Hotel in Bangkok, I was photographically seduced by a tree wrapped in neon fabric and festooned with Buddhas wearing floral necklaces. *(page 32)* I went ahead and shot before learning that the decorations were to appease the spirits dwelling in the tree. As for the enameled fruit in a Malaysian temple, I still don't have a clue what it's all about. *(preceding page)*

One fundamental reality check is to acknowledge that travel photography is not a specialty. In terms of subject matter, it is, in fact, the most diversified of fields. The destination photographer can address landscapes, fashions, lifestyles, architecture, nature, portraits, industry, cuisine, festivals, and crafts. It is impossible to take only one aesthetic approach to such diverse subjects. For this reason, it's difficult to develop a distinctive personal style as a travel photographer. Style is largely a by-product of selecting similar subject matter and treating it in a consistent fashion. Artists may pursue a variety of themes over the course of their career, but they generally do so in a serial fashion: they usually aren't continually changing subjects from one moment to the next. The travel photographer, on the other hand, confronts a person here, a marketplace there, a landmark around the corner, and a landscape down the road—all within a matter of minutes.

Beyond the formal challenge of establishing a unified stylistic approach to the endless variety of travel subjects, there is the difficulty of working in the studio of the world. The real world has no temperature control to cool off the Caribbean or warm up the Arctic. No CD player fills the shooting location with music of the photographer's choice. Models who never reject the camera or persistently ask for a tip are not available, nor can the travel photographer control the number of onlookers ogling him or her. Foul weather rolls in; no celestial strobe flashes down on the subject. The travel photographer can't take much time to contemplate a composition in the fluctuating real world; if you deliberate too long, a car parks in your picture.

Coordinating all the elements in a meaningful travel photograph is truly a challenge. Coming together simultaneously at 250th of a second as you press the shutter are intellectual, creative, technical, social, and physical factors.

Let's begin with the intellectual. The moment you are viscerally attracted to a subject, ask yourself what message you wish to convey. The intellectual content of a photograph is of critical importance in how well an image sustains prolonged viewing. The message or content of a photograph does not necessarily have to be journalistically expressed. An emotional quality might also be expressed in a more abstract way through color or texture. Nevertheless, it is important to know what you are trying to convey through the content of your photographs.

IT'S NO FUN lugging camera gear throughout London's theater district just in case a picture materializes. Inertia reinforced this lazy thought. But my husband, Landt, said he'd carry my tripod—an offer I was quick to accept. Naturally, a great shot of the *Miss Saigon* theater sign reflected in a window across the street materialized before my very eyes. And it wasn't the only shot I got that night. I've learned that the bright lights and glitter of theater districts are full of photo opportunities.

The creative factor is the soul of an image. Your creative inspiration is expressed in how you handle the aesthetic aspects of an image–the composition, color, texture, and light.

The technical factor is obvious–your selection of lens, filter, film, exposure, and all the other elements necessary for a technically excellent photograph. The intellectual and creative elements of a photograph are sacrificed without proper technique.

The social factor can easily be taken for granted in travel photography. Even if you are concentrating on inanimate subjects such as landmarks, landscapes, and still lifes, the chances for social interaction of some sort are high. Someone is always hanging around asking a question, needing to get past you, or telling you that you can't take the picture. It's hard, indeed, to sequester yourself from people when you're a travel photographer.

The physical factor is especially demanding. You may, for example, pound city pavements with a heavy camera bag and tripod and gear in a backpack. Finding dynamic new angles on traditional travel themes frequently requires exertion—even gymnastics. It can be exhausting work!

Regardless of these challenges, with every photograph you take, you must solve a variety of technical, aesthetic, and circumstantial problems. Your pictures are successful to the extent that solutions to these problems have been brought into a cooperative balance before the exposure is made. You will almost never have total control over the environment you're working in. Each photograph is a compromise between your creative aspirations, your expectations for the photo, the fixed realities of the subject, the technical parameters of your equipment, and the limitations of the shooting environment.

TRUE ABSTRACTION is hard to come by in unmanipulated photography. A straight photographic image is always a detail of something recognizable by someone. In Morocco, at the gilded gates of the Royal Palace in Fez, the setting sun created a strong shadow and a glistening effect on the door and surrounding tile work. With an 80–200mm zoom lens, I realized an approximation of abstraction in a minimal composition.

Despite the many problems to be solved with each picture you take, one factor usually stands out as the first or dominant challenge; this is the starting point from which all the other solutions are deduced. What mountaineering and landscape photographer Galen Rowell calls the "limiting factor" might be that you're not Icarus and can't fly across a chasm to get to a particular shooting angle on a mountain landscape. For me, the limiting factor might be that I'm not Superman and can't lift a garbage truck out of a city scene. There are any number of limiting technical factors as well, such as not having a long enough lens or fast enough film or a tripod at hand.

While the physical world is loaded with limitations for the travel photographer, it's my belief that the most aggressive and obdurate limiting factors are within our own heads and hearts. To master these personal limits, I've created a process that challenges the most commonly recurring of them. This process includes quelling disorientation, overcoming inertia, appreciating novel qualities, listening for creative clues, understanding personal style, giving in to visual seduction, developing cultural competence, and celebrating the exotic.

In her best-selling book *On Photography*, Susan Sontag writes: "It seems positively unnatural to travel without taking a camera along. . . . The very activity of taking pictures is soothing and assuages general feelings of disorientation that are likely to be exacerbated by travel." I believe this is true: even after thirty years as a professional travel photographer, I still feel a bit disoriented when I first arrive in a foreign country.

AMUSED BY A produce sign in rural France and struck by the contrast of the white-on-black letters, I heard inertia say, "That's not a picture! It's just a boring, black sign in the middle of nowhere." Yet the simplicity and charm of the sign offset by yellow mustard is precisely the point of the picture.

Not so concerned with my personal safety, my disorientation has more to do with whether the people in a country will be receptive to my photographic advances. Until I get into the swing of a culture, the anticipation of rejection makes my first steps tentative. As I begin taking photographs, the barrier drops; I feel more in control of myself and more comfortable in the foreign environment.

The opposite of this type of cultural atunement is the camera-as-shield syndrome. Sontag is also insightful on this common pitfall. She writes: "Most tourists feel compelled to put the camera between themselves and whatever is remarkable that they encounter. Unsure of other responses, they take a picture. This gives shape to experience: stop, take a photograph, and move on." Indeed, indiscriminate picture taking is a way of validating one's presence when one feels like a foreign invader. The photographic act punctuates the travel experience, giving it convenient form, if not meaning.

Overcoming photographic inertia is the next step in my creative process. The most subtle limiting factor, photographic inertia is how I describe all the arguments that try to scuttle my impulse to act on a picture possibility. These arguments range from I'm tired, it's raining, the film is too slow, the wrong lens is on the camera, the bus is waiting, my husband is restless to they'll ask for money, I'm not allowed in there, people are watching, I don't speak the language, I have no flash, I hate that color.

Once I've overcome these arguments and said yes to a subject, I can begin to actively appreciate it. Acknowledging the qualities of beauty, balance, mystery, or light that the subject contains is far more important to me than anticipating the great picture I'm going to get. After all, as a travel photographer dealing in a straight, unmanipulated mode of the medium, I don't create my subjects—I only recognize them with each exposure on film.

WHEN I BUILD compositions in from the edges, I pay more attention to the periphery of the frame than to what's in the middle of the picture. Untidy edges compromise otherwise good compositions. Edge control such as I achieved in this photo from the Taos Indian pueblo in New Mexico is difficult for those wearing glasses, who are unable to scan the edges with their eye distanced from the viewfinder. Using a diopter on the viewfinder or wearing contacts for shooting would be preferable.

Appreciation leads directly into the listening phase. As I begin working on a subject, I raise my antennae for both creative and technical clues that are coming to me through common sense and intuition. In order to hear these clues, it's necessary to disregard external environmental static, including time pressures, onlookers making me self-conscious, the threat that the situation will change before I'm ready to shoot, being in a dangerous spot, running out of film, dealing with interruptions from passersby, and so on.

Internal environmental static must also be lowered, including anxiety over the outcome of the picture, concern that the image reflect my creative aspirations, cultural disorientation induced by a strange place, and fluctuations in the physical and emotional energy that is needed to cope with photographing in a challenging foreign culture.

Once you've cleared the airwaves of internal and external static, the clues come through almost audibly. I hear them directing the picture-taking as if by remote control, with tips like use a different lens, make it a vertical, shift to the left, get in closer, bracket the exposure.

Sometimes I hear, "Sack it! This is a no-win situation; abandon the shot altogether and move on!" I really fight this directive; if I tune it out and end up with a bad picture, I can always throw it away—the picture is merely a reminder of my lack of good judgment at the time of exposure. But a crucial part of the listening phase is to pay attention to your judgment. You may feel that the subject really isn't worth your time and film. Or you may feel that immovable objects in the scene truly hinder your ability to make a good image—the picture will be compromised. So, be willing to walk away from a nominal subject.

Having determined the composition, I pay attention to cues on how to handle the most minute details within the frame. For example, a cigarette butt or a

plastic bag may need to be removed. I'm obsessed with correcting elements within the frame that I consider to be off by so much as a millimeter; a successful image is in the details. Remember that you don't have to take the world the way it dishes itself out to you. The world is the raw material for artistic expression, and if a picture can be improved by fixing the collar on a subject's jacket or removing an ash can, do it.

GRAPHIC SIMPLICITY can capture the destination photographer at every turn. On a street corner in Roussillon, a Provençal hill town in France, I stopped to consider the light and shadow on the walls, punctuated by the street plaque and No Parking signs. I decided the scene was worth a try, and using average metering, I bracketed the exposure at both full and half-stop increments to get a good compromise in the highlight and shadow detail.

An important part of this precision phase is to scrutinize the edges of the viewfinder for unwanted or distracting elements. It's not enough to center a primary point of interest in the viewfinder and have messy edges. In classes at Harvard, author John Updike likens writing to the making of a good sandwich: "Butter toward the edges," he says. "Enough gets in the middle anyway."

Knowing that travel photographs are apt to be center intensive, largely due to the "point and shoot" approach engendered by autofocus cameras, I try to tighten up around the edges as much as possible. Learn to devote more attention to edge control than to what's smack in the middle of the composition.

Watching the edges is, however, difficult for those who wear glasses. If you can, wear contacts when you're shooting, or install a diopter in the camera so you can get your eye right up to the eyepiece of the viewfinder. Also, most cameras only let you see from 93 to 97 percent of what will end up on a slide. Know your camera's limitations in this regard, and to control edges, compensate by moving in a bit closer to your subjects.

Finally, before you shoot, double-check your overall composition to make sure it's what you intended from the start. I always ask myself whether I wish to alter it somewhat. This is especially important with handheld shots, when you must take the camera away from your eye to make adjustments to the subject. With tripod shots, you can leave the established camera several times to make the adjustments. In so doing, you might kick the tripod or the weight of a telephoto lens might cause the camera to slip on the tripod head. Remember to always check these things before exposing film.

AN OLD-WORLD wrought-iron security gate caught my eye in Nice. At first, I framed up the entire gate—and the windows and the wires and the drain-pipe. It was too much. Finally, I paid attention and zeroed in with an 80–200mm zoom lens on the wrought-iron S-curve and classic shutters for a tighter, more lyrical composition of Matisse's Old Nice.

Critical to the creative process is understanding your fundamental sense of structure and balance. This is revealed by a characteristic attraction to either symmetry or asymmetry, which manifests itself in every aspect of your life. You may fluctuate between the two impulses, but one or the other will be the dominant governing force. For example, I know that I am governed mainly by symmetry. I'm more attracted to the symmetrical architecture of a Palladian villa than I am to the asymmetrical arrangement of rocks in a Zen garden. I can still relate to Kyoto's Rioan-ji garden, but the Villa Rotunda in Vicenza resonates more profoundly for me.

Understanding your design orientation, you can approach the issues of composition with greater confidence. This is where intuitive composition comes from—call it karmic composition! With practice, you will learn to focus on subjects that naturally submit to your creative preferences. Eventually, a style will emerge, as common themes and consistent aesthetic treatments accumulate in your work.

Before you develop this confidence, of course, the rules of composition taught in art schools and photo classes can serve as guides. The compositional canons are, no doubt, familiar: for example, organize a composition into thirds, don't put horizon lines in the middle of a picture, look for leading lines entering a composition from its edges, don't place the principal subject of interest in the middle of a composition.

Using both subjective preferences and general aesthetic guidelines, it is possible to develop a stylistic signature as a travel photographer. And technical tools can help as well. For example, one of my workshop students—a successful banker—was frustrated by an almost hopeless sense of photographic composition. Because composition and style are intertwined, it occurred to me to install an architectural grid in her viewfinder. With its faint grid of squares etched on the glass, the screen aids in organizing elements in the viewfinder. With her quantitative mind, the banker could then work on composition by thinking about percentages and ratios with the aid of the grid. This way she could aesthetically translate her native compositional tendencies into her image making.

SPONTANEITY IS definitely part of the creative process in destination photography. On Jamaica, I outwitted a request for a tip with a totally unexpected, spontaneous response. I was about to shoot a boat under a reed shelter when a guy from out of nowhere claimed it was his boat and that I had to pay him for the picture. "It's Sunday," I said lightly. "The guidebook says pictures are free on Sunday in Jamaica." He had probed, I had parried. We laughed, he left. I got the shot.

Anyone can find a personal compositional or style key. If you love color, investigate its attributes intellectually and philosophically, then translate the investigation onto film. If you appreciate music, consider harmony and rhythm through the viewfinder. Developing style in travel photography, as in any art form, means recognizing and expressing particular qualities. Thus, it's necessary to determine what qualities of thought and character you want to bring out in your own life—and therefore in your photography. Style evolves from the intelligent quest for a clear and appropriate presentation of these qualities. This relationship between character and style underscores the belief held by many photographers that photography is truly an autobiographical medium—style is not mere gesture, but rather a personal metaphor. As Don Carroll and Quentin Crisp wrote in their book, *Doing It With Style,* "Style is an idiom which arises spontaneously from one's personality, but which is deliberately maintained. To be a stylist is to be yourself—on purpose."

THE CONCEPT of "gesture" is often discussed in the rarefied world of fine arts. Gesture is any body movement that conveys an emotion or intent. In a photographic image, capturing subtle or dramatic gesture adds impact to any picture. In India, the frequent palm-up gesture needs no explanation for either locals or tourists. Here I was struck by the beauty of this beggar's gesture set off by stunning color in the flat light.

The ultimate goal, of course, is to stop obsessing about style. The fun really begins when you become one with the camera, when you begin to see without doubting your vision and can give spontaneous photographic form to feeling. The most fun I have as a travel photographer is giving way to a visual seduction. As a photographer traveling the world over, I find that third-world countries provide myriad visually seductive subjects for my camera. However, it took me a while to learn to respond to them. In exotic places like Chiang Mai, Samarkand, Chengdu, Timbuktu, Bukhara, and Kathmandu, I would find myself staring at something weird and wonderful, transfixed by a peculiar manifestation of local culture. With my camera dangling and my eyes riveted, inspiration would urge me to go for it, but my mind would remain nonplussed. The camera would continue to dangle.

As a travel photographer, I had to overcome our tendency to respond to the known and knowable, to imagery that supports our expectations of a place. These expectations are generally based on images acquired through the work of friends or from photographs published in travel magazines and tourism brochures; they are limited by the perception, imagination, and experience of their photographers, whether professional or amateur. While these orthodox shots certainly have merit, the more unique sights seldom make it onto film, let alone onto the published page. Yet for me, it's the images that are visually seductive, that elicit the question "What is it?" that prove to be the strongest lure in travel photography: the more weird and exotic, the better.

Especially in the more exotic cultures, cultural competence is essential to creative travel photography. My friend Merle Lefkoff, a conflict-resolution facilitator with global experience, defines cultural competence as "the ability to live and work in social and cultural diversity and to form productive alliances. Cultural competence is not intellectual or skill based; it is intuitive and existential." Defined as such, cultural competence engenders a kind of spontaneity that ameliorates the flat-footed, invasive attributes that so often attend travel photography. This social finesse allows for travelers who value multicultural experiences. They are motivated more by the formation of alliances through the photographic experience, no matter how brief, than by the token shots they would get as standard camera-toting tourists.

Returning once more to Diana Vreeland, I recall the 1993 retrospective at the Costume Institute of the Metropolitan Museum of Art titled "Diana Vreeland: Immoderate Style." There, the curators had listed qualities attributed to Diana Vreeland. The one that caught my eye was "Exoticism: A global, culturally pluralistic vision of beauty."

To me, creativity and the traveling eye have everything to do with developing and extolling exoticism—in life as well as on film.

A COMMON travel conundrum is when a nonphotographing spouse or companion starts calling the shots. At the Palace Museum in Jaipur my husband, Landt, pointed out a red bag hanging from the ceiling of the colonnade. "You're nuts," I said. "Nobody will know what it is." But I went on to take the picture, and it turned out to be a pivotal shot: this chandelier covered in a pigeon-proof bag stimulated my visual appetite for more weird and wonderful travel images. *(above)*

PRECISION WAS the name of the game when photographing these two girls on South Sulawesi in Indonesia. Originally I moved in on the girl on the left with a 60mm macro lens. As I did so, the other girl leaned her head shyly on her friend's shoulder. The batik cloth covering her head fell over one eye, and I instantly recognized the potential for a one-of-a-kind image. I precisely composed the other girl's face, framing just along the nose to achieve this rhythmic Indonesian portrait. *(right)*

ONE OF THE most creative attitudes we can adopt is the acceptance of reality. What's real about the third world is its increasing westernization. A good example is the shot I took with a 20mm lens of a Buddhist monk's hot socks and sneakers at a Nepalese stupa at sixteen thousand feet above sea level. *(above)* Even these guys get to market in Kathmandu once a year or more. On Bali, when I saw an Indonesian teenager wearing a Wrangler T-shirt, I just stared at the sartorial incongruity. Of course, the cross-cultural fashion statement is precisely the point of the picture I took with a 60mm macro lens. *(opposite)*

THE TRAVELER'S EYE

DEVELOPING A SURE SENSE of composition takes lots of practice. An opportunity to coordinate compositions presented itself to me at a bus stop at Guatemala's Solola market. While they waited to take a bus home, women had taken their shopping baskets from their heads and placed them down on a ledge along the street. Here was an ideal opportunity to coordinate a variety of compositions shooting the baskets at different focal lengths. The first shot seemed too wide to me, so I moved in closer to include only three of the baskets. A few feet away, I tried horizontal and vertical compositions of another grouping that coordinated a green, blue, and white patch of painted wall into the compositions. The women were amused until the bus driver honked his departure for the hinterlands. The baskets were popped back onto heads as they scurried to climb on board. *(pages 48–49)*

CAPTURING AMERICANA can be an exercise in photographic kitsch. A deer-decorated wheel cover on the back of a vehicle was perfect prey for my wide-angle lens treatment in Ouray, Colorado, including the town's Victorian architecture. *(above)* When ticketed by a New Mexican policeman for speeding, I struggled in asking the officer if I could . . . shoot his gun—frame up his firearm—take his pistol; it all sounded bad. He got the picture; I got mine—and the ticket too. *(left)*

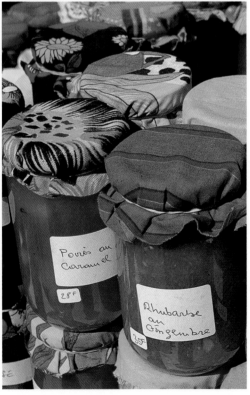

FRANCE PROVIDES a strong feeling-of-place, especially Provence, which exists at the crossroads of soul, sophistication, and sensuality. At the market in Old Nice, I organized a composition with a 28mm lens that maximized the pattern between a woman's flowers and umbrella. *(opposite)* In the Luberon Valley, I took market detail shots with a 60mm macro lens of vinegar bottles, jam jars, and fabrics, all symbols of the French lifestyle. *(this page)*

TRAVEL PHOTOGRAPHY is highly social. Children appear from nowhere when you think you've got the landscape to yourself. While recording a door, it suddenly opens. Practically every photograph you take these days involves some degree of interaction with locals, even when the shot is of an inanimate subject. At Santa Fe's annual Indian market, for example, every shot of the artists' works required asking permission, often resulting in lengthy conversation. *(above)* In Antigua, Guatemala, I became a mime to make the appropriate nonverbal and non-monetary connection with the mother before I went for a picture of her baby wrapped in swaddling clothes. *(right)*

STYLE IS THE by-product of consistently choosing similar subject matter and treating it in a consistent aesthetic fashion. Given the diverse subject matter the travel photographer deals with, personal style is hard to come by. You can't handle, optically or aesthetically, landscapes and architecture in the same way as portraits or ethnic dances. To the extent that I have developed a personal style in my destination photography, I've done so, in part, by suspending preconceived notions of what constitutes a viable travel image. On a Nepalese trek, a Hindu shrine to the goddess Shiva made of lingam stones is as viable a shot as the Himalayan landscape. *(above)* In Chichicastenango, women's shopping bags parked on a restaurant pole and a child's grubby feet surrounded by votive rose petals on the church steps constitute travel-photo fodder and reflect my style. *(left and opposite)*

IN TRAVEL photography, identifying the qualities of attraction is key to a conscious creative process. A photograph may express a wide variety of qualities: beauty, humor, grace, charm, rhythm, exoticism, symmetry, color, texture, light, or mystery. By recognizing these qualities in the world's raw material, we essentially recognize them in ourselves, as well. It's like seeing from the inside out. In Guatemala, I was attracted by the rhythm and beauty expressed in the embroidered man's jacket, which I captured by aiming up with a 60mm macro lens. *(above)* In Kenya, I was struck by the exoticism and humor of these Samburu dancers' mix of ethnic jewelry and Western watches. I asked them to hold their hands together so I could consolidate the qualities in a composition made with a 35–70mm zoom lens set at about 50mm. *(right)*

AESTHETIC EXERCISES

....

IN AN INTERVIEW WITH *DARKROOM* magazine, Ansel Adams said, "I haven't really changed my point of view for many years. I'm still doing about the same thing I started in 1927." Curiously enough, he goes on to say, "Now, if I had a new concept tomorrow, I would be very happy."

Personally, I'd be very unhappy if I didn't have new concepts on a regular basis requiring various photographic treatments. I simply do not want to take the same photograph for a lifetime. I agree with Picasso when he said that a personal style can become a rut. To avoid stylistic ruts, I find self-assignments to be very useful.

Shortly after arriving in a destination, I will conceive of an aesthetic or technical exercise in which I will concentrate on a particular subject or theme throughout the trip. I'll take other, unrelated shots as well; concentrating on a visual theme is not mutually exclusive with general coverage of a destination. But instead of just wandering around, aimlessly looking for isolated images, I more quickly uncover a sense of place with a self-assignment.

I distill the essence of a destination by exploring how my self-assignment can best be conveyed photographically. Besides maintaining an alertness throughout the trip to images that carry out the theme of the exercise, the self-assignment prevents visual ennui after the initial excitement of arriving has worn off. I find I am compelled to respond more personally and definitely to situations if I am playing with this visual or narrative thread.

A self-assignment flexes aesthetic muscles—you get valuable visual stimulation by treating subjects or themes in various ways. But not only do stylistic muscles need exercise, so do mental muscles. Self-assignments require intellectual focus. As Joel Meyerowitz told *American Photographer* magazine, "Photography is a revelatory form. What you photograph shows you what you're really interested in. And, if you can be in touch with yourself that way, you'll always see what's necessary for you."

THE WATER POTS OF India are, I found, a visually appealing symbol of the country, and so offered me a subject for one of my aesthetic self-assignments. *(pages 60–61)*

I COULD HAPPILY photograph every fall in Arles's atmospheric Place du Forum. In seasonal transition, the plane trees drop their leaves all over the ground and they float onto classic French café chairs. One of my objectives with self-assignments is to try out a variety of focal lengths, and so at the Café la Nuit, I made an establishing shot of the statue of poet Frédéric Mistral with an 80–200mm lens on a tripod, a 24mm image of a wicker chair collecting leaves, and various other compositions with a 35–70mm zoom lens. *(pages 63–65)*

THE TRAVELER'S EYE

FOR MY self-assignment in Rajasthan, I became an ardent pot watcher, seeking them out in as wide a variety of locations and situations as I could find. Pictures of pots made of clay, copper, aluminum, and brass, found in country and city markets, at fairs, by the Ganges, and in palaces, composed a single body of work and were a welcome change from my unrelated Indian shots. *(this page and opposite)*

ENVIRONMENTAL
TRAVEL
PORTRAITS

....

E
NDING HER CAREER AS THE DIRECTOR
of the Metropolitan Museum's Fashion Institute, the late Diana Vreeland
appreciated the caretaking role of curators, noting that "the intensity of maintaining a beautiful ribbon or arranging it on a sleeve was given as much attention in the eighteenth century as an artisan would give to the arabesque curve
of a ceiling. Marie Antoinette had a curator of laces, also a curator of ribbons."

Curators—this is what we are as travel portrait photographers. When people abroad allow us to take their photograph, they give themselves over to our

curatorial trust. Adjusting their "laces and ribbons" is not effrontery; it is a privilege and a necessary part of portrait photography. No matter how high or humble, foreign or familiar, if approached with unself-conscious spontaneity, people are comfortable as we photograph them. When we are free ourselves, our subjects feel free to be themselves in front of our camera.

How do you convey to people that they can trust you as a person and as a photographer? Taking curatorial control is part of the answer. Know why you have chosen a subject and have a reasonably clear idea of how you intend to treat the photograph *before* you make an approach. Nothing creates distrust, unease, and impatience more quickly than allowing a photographer to take a picture of you, then seeing him fumble for a different lens, take time figuring out the exposure, and cast about for a better background. I always get myself organized technically and aesthetically before I go up to a subject; it is a prerequisite to gracefully executing travel portraits.

It is also important to use curatorial judgment in the choice of subjects. Many photographers I've observed on foreign photo tours simply snap at anyone who'll agree to being photographed, oblivious to ugly backgrounds and bad lighting.

I ELIMINATE undesirable backgrounds from portrait shots by moving in with a macro lens. With the close-focusing capability of the macro lens, I can crop in on someone's head and fill the frame with their features from a distance of only a few inches. Some of my fledgling attempts to move in on portraits occurred on Guadeloupe. There, I took a colorful portrait of a smiling Creole chef at the annual Fête des Cuisinières *(page 68)*, and one of a small boy *(preceding page)*. Not liking the boy's surroundings—a doorway with plastic streamers—I asked the boy to hold the streamers in his hands. As I eased in with a 60mm macro, the streamers took on an unexpectedly strong aesthetic importance.

Critical judgment as to whether the subject is really interesting or photogenic is often neglected, resulting in ordinary people pictures that lack compositional rigor.

The first thing you should think about when you are photographically attracted to a person is the environment. Travel portraits, in fact, are often "environmental" portraits, since the foreign environment can be as important as the person, conveying information about the subject's culture, activities, and surroundings.

In order to include as much as possible of a subject's environment, I often use wide-angle lenses, 24mm or 28mm, for stylized environmental portraits. I'm not concerned about distorting the subject, since in most of my environmental portraits, the subjects are not that close to the lens. Besides, I'm not trying to make perfect, undistorted likenesses of them anyway, since my photographs aren't going to end up on their piano. As Richard Avedon once said, "A portrait is not a likeness. The moment an emotion or fact is transformed into a photograph, it is no longer a fact but an opinion. There is no such thing as accuracy in a photograph. All photographs are inaccurate. None of them is the truth."

I seldom shoot an environmental travel portrait without first "styling" the picture. I'll manipulate the subjects, moving them to a better background, adjusting their clothing, removing extraneous objects, directing the pose, and orchestrating their expression. I accomplish this degree of cooperation by conveying that sense of curatorial trust. People sense that you are not after a hit-and-run snap—like the last tourist they rejected. If they see you really trying to take a good picture, many people get caught up in the process, respect it—even find it fun. In fact, I don't feel I'm "taking" pictures of people. A lot of giving goes into the kind of cross-cultural photographic experience I'm talking about.

Photographing people is undoubtedly more of a challenge today than it was years ago. Even in the most remote parts of the world, people are overwhelmed by the sheer number of

WHENEVER I want to photograph a vendor in a market, I marshal myself and my cameras before going up to them. It must be annoying to allow a foreigner to take your picture only to have them fuss around, changing lenses and angles, while shoppers queue up. Seeking photos in French markets, like the fabulous produce market in Old Nice where I recorded this fisherman, always nets me good portraits.

tourists aiming still and video cameras at them. More and more, people simply refuse to be subjects, wagging their fingers and shaking their heads firmly. This is understandable: if all the people in the tourist hot spots of the world stopped to pose for everyone who wanted a picture, their lives would come to a standstill.

In response to the inevitable refusals, I suggest that you learn to not take it personally—simply smile and move on. Quality in portrait photography is, after all, more important than quantity. I take fewer people pictures today than I did even five years ago. Although more people are saying no or asking for money, I don't get discouraged or annoyed. Nor do I become a Lady Bountiful, reaching for spare change. I simply place higher demands on myself; I don't mind if I come home from a trip with only a few wonderful pictures of people.

Because I'm not interested in plundering the world for images of exotic folks

in remote cultures, I try hard to approach my travel portraiture as an individual photographing individuals. Rather than pressing myself on a foreign culture the way I used to do, I have learned that people pictures will come my way naturally. There will always be people who enjoy having their picture taken, regardless of the local beliefs about photography. Seek out individuals who will recognize your own individuality and who won't condemn you automatically to the rank of tourist. Let these people become your subjects; they are willing to do a foreigner a favor, with no strings attached.

I TAKE ALL the do's and don'ts in travel guides with a grain of salt. Often the caveats regarding people photography published in guides only reflect the author's lack of cultural competence. While photographing women in Arab cultures can be a challenge, I've always found exceptions to local rules prohibiting it. These Moroccan women, for example, put up no resistance to my photographing them, and the men standing around didn't police the situation, either.

Just as the dedicated travel photographer hopes not to be dismissed by locals as a typical tourist, it is important for the visitor not to be overwhelmed by exoticism; we must never view indigenous people as curiosities in a global zoo. A strange emotional confusion can arise in photographers stemming from the sheer differences in economic living standards around the world. For example, frequently in my travels I encounter people who are much richer than I am, but I don't expect them to feel sorry for me. Similarly I try to avoid emotional blackmail when I'm traveling in countries where many people are poor by Western standards—I cannot focus on the individuality of my subjects through a veil of tears. This does not mean that I'm blind and insensitive to poverty, but I don't allow this awareness to block the possibilities of a cross-cultural experience—no one is the richer for that.

V. S. Naipaul addresses this type of confusion in *An Area of Darkness* when he writes: "Therefore, to see its [India's] poverty is to make an observation of no value. Do not think that your anger and contempt are marks of your sensitivity. You might have seen more: the smiles on the faces of the begging children, that domestic group among the pavement sleepers waking in the cool Bombay morning, father, mother, and baby in a trinity of love, so self-contained that they are as private as if walls had separated them from you: it is your gaze that violates them, your sense of outrage that outrages them . . . it is your surprise, your anger that denies [them] humanity."

Free from emotional blackmail, you can ensure that the photographic encounter is a positive one for your subjects. It begins with your approach. People often express a great deal of anxiety about approaching subjects photographically. Frequently, photographers will say that they feel as though they are

imposing on and taking advantage of others. Well, you *are* imposing when you wander up to someone with a camera. That person has to stop whatever he or she is doing to entertain your photographic request. But are you necessarily a negative imposition? You might actually be a pleasant or amusing experience; you might even alleviate the boredom of the day. The important thing is to make your request respectfully and sincerely, and with your self-esteem intact.

Approaching people for photographs requires a real desire to make cross-cultural connections. The encounter should also include the discipline of expressing gratitude. Genuine gratitude—not obsequiousness—is, I feel, an essential lesson to learn in taking portraits of people. I often see

ON A PRESS trip in Malaysia, I set up a portrait of a kite maker. While I worked up close with a 20mm lens, other photographers shot my subject from in back of me and over my shoulders. Although I was too polite to shoo them away, on my own travel photography tours, I insist that there be no interference, please! Whoever has done the work to establish photo rapport with a subject deserves to be left alone.

participants on photo tours enter fairly well into a photographic encounter with someone, but their exit leaves much to be desired. They depart with little acknowledgment of the person who has just posed for them, leaving the subject bewildered by the hit-and-run shooter. Perfunctory thanks are not enough and should leave any sensitive photographer with an accumulating sense of cultural and personal indebtedness.

These days, getting travel portraits requires much more than simply "being nice." Superficial attempts to ingratiate yourself into getting people pictures just don't work anymore. Most people in the heavily traveled parts of the world are tired of the cheery-tourist tactic. Instead we, as photographers, must transcend being nice to simply being—being human, being natural, being ourselves.

Sounds facile? It isn't! The "be nice" approach is the facile one. It is also manipulative and carries with it the will to overwhelm subjects photographically. Try just "being," without placing any personal demands on a culture. Try divesting yourself of acquisitiveness for people pictures; stop caring if you get any good portraits today. Let them come to you free of angst.

Learn to rely on a sort of cross-cultural free association. Wandering through exotic markets bustling with wonderfully photogenic people, you may discover that your subjects actually choose you, rather than the reverse, if you remain open to the moment. This kind of free association engages serendipity and allows your connections to come more easily and naturally. It also helps to minimize the stress that frequently accompanies travel photography in general.

Despite the difficulties, there's no doubt in my mind that photographing people is the most satisfying area of travel photography. The landscapes are lovely and the architecture's grand, but back home, you will be richer for the cross-cultural experiences you've had while photographing people. Being led to your subjects is what is so fascinating. You may even come to value the experience of the photo encounter more than the celluloid trophy: the experience will remain in your memory long after you have tired of the picture.

UNDER CERTAIN conditions, distortion is not a problem when using a wide-angle lens for portraits. In Nepal, I used a 24mm lens for this portrait of a woman. Framing in quite close, I achieved a sense of optical intimacy that would not have been possible using a longer-focal-length lens. Keeping her face toward the middle of the frame, where the distortion is least apparent, I took advantage of the dimensionality produced by wide-angle optics: the woman is clearly separated from the background. *(opposite)*

GOOD BACKGROUNDS for portraits are often hard to come by. When necessary, I will literally buy them. At Guadeloupe's Fête des Cuisinières, these Creole chefs were the island's culinary queens for the day. Knowing that the festival would take place in an ugly cement schoolyard, I purchased several fabrics with island motifs to tape on a shaded wall near the festivities. Bringing a stool from my hotel for the ladies to sit on in my on-location studio, I waited with my camera on a tripod while my husband, Landt, asked various chefs to pose for me. *(left top)*

WHEN A photograph appears in my mind's eye, I try to take control to make the image happen. Needing to eliminate an unphotogenic environment in Guatemala, I envisioned three women creating a body-block background so I could pose children in various ways in front of their textiled torsos. Feeling free to rearrange the elements to conform to my creative impulses, I up the aesthetic ante: I can no longer blame the world for its visual shortcomings. *(left bottom)*

THE TRAVELER'S EYE

TO EXPAND MY definition of travel portraiture, I'll concentrate on a detail of a person's face or clothing at the expense of a whole head shot. Resembling a fashion treatment, perhaps, rather than a traditional travel snap, my travel portraits are more often about national style than they are about the actual person. Beefeaters' uniforms at the Queen's Day Parade in London, for instance, provided a sartorial study, *(opposite top)* while a Mexican teenager's screaming lipstick and macabre nail polish became a south-of-the-border fashion statement *(opposite bottom)*.

TO COMMUNICATE with my pilgrim portrait subject at the Taj Mahal, it was mime over matter. I mimed my way through getting him to sit on a bench, rotate his body toward the camera, and look toward the rising sun. I pulled the cloth back over his head when it fell off. Then I negotiated the camera angle to make sure the turret didn't rise out of the middle of his head. Made with a 24mm lens, this environmental portrait is a long-standing favorite of mine. *(above)*

WALKING INTO a rug shop in Morocco, I noted that the decorative painting in the vestibule would be a great background for a portrait. The shop owner was the perfect, willing candidate. Using a tripod and a 28mm lens, I asked a fellow traveler to hold a LiteDisc reflector outside and bounce auxiliary light into the man's face while I shot. A round reflector that curls up into a small diameter, the LiteDisc is an indispensable tool when you need to kick up the light level a bit. *(above)*

IMPOSE ON people? Of course! We are always imposing on people when we ask them to pose for us. You can be a positive imposition, however. An old lady selling lace in a Yugoslav market probably rarely had so much fun or attention as when I took her portrait. A crowd gathered around to cheer her on. A positive presentation on the photographer's part and a little grace go a long way in providing pleasurable, noninvasive photographic encounters with local folks on your travels. *(opposite)*

A STUDENT AT one of my workshops admitted she was unnerved by the inscrutable stares from the dark eyes of many Indians. But in India, eyes are what I thrive on photographically. Centuries of spiritual discipline and stillness seem to penetrate the emulsion every time I expose film on people such as this camel herder at the Pushkar Fair, taken with a 60mm macro lens. *(opposite)*

AT INDIA'S Pushkar Fair, I was photographing a man, turbaned and swathed in a glorious red cloth. As I framed him up through the viewfinder, I realized that even in all his glory he wasn't enough to stand alone as portrait. Fortunately, his pals were sitting in the sand watching me try to figure out a better approach. It was obvious—include the other men in an intimate arrangement. *(above)*

THE TRAVELER'S EYE

AT MY WORKSHOP, I'm always asked, "How did you get that shot?" In an attempt to get a good portrait of an Indian woman, I took a sequence of shots that illustrates my progression from original vision to resolution on film. At first, I was magnetized by the way the woman carrying a baby held her sari in her mouth, watching me with one eye as I feigned photographic interest in the water pots. Assessing the light, I realized I'd have to move the mother to the left of the pots so the sun could shine more directly onto her face. Asking the women to move, I took a polite overall shot of the group. Then I moved in with a 60mm macro lens for an eye-to-eye shot of the mother. Placing her face toward the left of the frame to avoid the baby, I was finally ready to shoot when she smiled, dropping the sari from her mouth. I remained composed and took a couple shots while considering how to regain my original vision. I gently reached out and took the sari in my hand and drew it across the woman's face. She got the message and took the sari in hand. Back on track, we were seeing eye-to-eye.

IN NORTH YEMEN, I had no interest in photographing this rug until I saw nearby an old man wearing a color-coordinated orange turban. I asked the man to pose, gesturing toward the rug. He stood directly in front of it. To convey what I wanted, I actually took his cane and squatted down myself. Framing the scene, I realized that the rug stopped at the left, revealing an ugly cement wall. I then drew into the picture the rug-shop owner who was watching with amusement this Western woman push his Arab brother around. The shopkeeper's dagger fell perfectly into the composition and he never knew he wasn't entirely in the shot. *(above)*

I THINK OF an environmental portrait as one in which elements in the photograph tell the viewer about an individual's life, culture, work, hobbies, or idiosyncrasies. A wool merchant's shop in Essaouira, Morocco, presented a perfect setting for such a portrait. I used a tripod in low light and a 24mm lens to exaggerate the wool hanging on the door. With the shallow depth-of-field that I got at a one-quarter-second shutter speed at f5.6, the door is not sharp. In this case the softness of the foreground directs the eye to the man, who is sharply revealed in the recesses of his shop. *(opposite)*

TRAVEL PHOTO-JOURNALISM

ONE OF THE BEST CLASSROOMS FOR photography in general is a job on a daily newspaper. From 1968 to 1970 I was one of the first female news photographers in the country on a major metropolitan newspaper as a staffer for the *Boston Globe*. There I learned that photojournalistic images are those in which a story is told with as little intervention as possible from the photographer. Usually the pictures are taken in a quick, surreptitious fashion. Ideally, the people in your viewfinder are not aware of being recorded. If they have noticed, you wait for them to resume their activity in a natural fashion before continuing to shoot.

Getting successful photojournalistic photographs largely depends on having quick visual and physical reflexes. Capturing peak action, or the "decisive moment" as Cartier Bresson called it, is a matter of staying visually alert to what is going on. You must also be prepared to act the moment events take place. It's a matter of coordination of the mind, body, and camera, and it takes lots of practice. Some photographers are more attuned to this approach to travel photography than are others—it's a very individual matter.

DEEP IN THE Fez souk, where one deals with all manner of mysterious and tricky Moroccan light, I spot-metered off the highlight in a rug hanging on a wall. Then I hung out for the right figure to enter the frame. In this hit-or-miss situation, I shot lots of film of many passer-by to optimize getting the right silhouette in the right place at the right time. A motor drive helps with the odds, as well. *(page 88)*

To be good, a journalistic image must respect angle and composition as much as it captures the decisive moment. For example, if there is an ongoing activity like people buying and selling in a market, don't shoot right off the bat. Ask yourself, do I have the best angle to get a clear recording of the specific action? At what point will the action be at its peak and have the most impact in the composition? Is the background better from across the street?

As you compose the subject and scrutinize the edges of the frame, look out for distracting elements. Quell your eagerness to start shooting long enough to consider the elements that make a good image. It's not enough to get the action squat in the middle of the viewfinder with no regard to the entire composition.

IN INDIA, I enjoy photographing both men and women as they deport themselves with saris, shoulder coverings, and turbans. Men unwind and rewind their turbans, depositing snakes of fabric on the floor. Women drop their saris in bright puddles on the ground while they rearrange their hair or undergarments. With this imagery in mind, I knew I was in for a good shot when I spotted a Gandhi-like man flipping his airy, cotton shawl around. *(preceding page)*

Don't compromise the picture out of impulsiveness and anxiety.

If you sense you don't have time for all these computations, go ahead and take a couple quick shots—get the happening on film. Then if circumstances allow, keep shooting to work out the flaws. The biggest mistake amateurs make is not exposing enough film as the action evolves.

Another common flaw of journalistic travel photographs is camera motion during exposure. Especially when using a handheld telephoto lens, you must hold the camera steady! Be sure you are supporting the barrel with one hand. Don't have both hands on the camera body, leaving the lens flopping in space. If you are vulnerable to camera motion, use a fast enough shutter speed to minimize it.

A fast shutter speed is also important for previsualized action shots. I frequently discover a background I really like. Having composed the picture and determined the exposure, I'll stake myself out across the street with a 28–85mm zoom lens or hang around even closer with a 25mm wide-angle. I'll photograph the local residents as they walk past my chosen background, but only when they

enter the portion of the frame that makes for the best composition. It usually takes 250th of a second to stop action that is moving laterally across the film plane. This does not mean, however, that action must always be stopped. Women in colorful blurred saris streaking across an ancient Indian wall can be a wonderfully artistic treatment. Whatever the approach, you must be technically prepared to capture the action you visualize. If you're not, all art is lost.

As a travel photographer, I no longer consider myself a photojournalist. Certainly, some of my images are photojournalistic and I enjoy them as much as other kinds of pictures. But ideally photojournalism and truth telling should be concomitant. If I were driven by my original journalistic instincts to uncover facts and reveal

THE TELEPHOTO lens is the principal tool of many travel photojournalists. It enables one to shoot people on the sly, hopefully without giving offense or being caught. On a Malaysian beach, I quickly snapped these two women deep in conversation to ensure getting them on film before they noticed me. Free and clear, I then refined the composition, placing the women toward the bottom of the frame to include more stripes in the boat.

truths about contemporary travel, many of my pictures would never be published in travel magazines and books. There, to promote tourism, editors and art directors focus on the sunny side of destinations. To be journalistically honest—or even balanced—has never been the intent of professional, commercial travel photography. And amateur destination photographers understandably strive to preserve pleasant holiday memories on film. Why shouldn't they!

"KEEP SHOOTING" is my motto. In a Moroccan tea shop two men paid no attention to me as I shot away with an 80–200mm lens. Hand-holding the camera in low light, I planted my elbows on a table and squeezed off thirtieth-of-a-second exposures. I exposed lots of film in between sips of mint tea to get images that were sharp enough and to capture a variety of expressions and gestures on the man facing me.

MANY TRAVEL photojournalistic opportunities require high-speed film, including this shot of the Day of the Dead observances in Oaxaca, Mexico. To capture the candlelit graveside vigils that go on throughout the night, I used a tripod, a fast 85mm f1.4 lens, and a film speed of ISO 800. The increased graininess and yellow cast from the candles add to the mood. *(above)*

UNDER TIGHT time pressures, news photojournalists are sometimes tempted to "fake" shots. Right or wrong, I reconstructed a basically journalistic shot of Jamaican coffee-plantation workers playing dominoes. I reoriented the domino chain and added the gas lantern and coffee cups to add light and tell the story better. The ethics of alteration may have to do with the difference between reporting the news accurately and conveying visual information. *(opposite)*

IN PARIS, lovers are fair game for the travel photographer. I was shooting the new I. M. Pei pyramid entrance to the Louvre when I spied this couple carrying on by the reflecting pool. With the camera on a tripod, I swung it around to capture them with an 80–200mm zoom lens. The couple looked at me and smiled. I waved back. As they continued their flirtation, a little girl entered the scene to ogle them, doubling the fun. *(above)*

WITH FEW Frenchmen wearing berets these days, especially in Paris, I knew I wanted this classic shot of an old-timer reading the paper in the Jardin du Luxembourg. Spotting the couple coming along, I waited and shot after they had entered the scene. Motor-driven exposures gave me options as to where the couple looked best in the composition. *(opposite)*

MAGIC MOMENTS in travel photojournalism often occur during spiritual observances in churches, temples, and mosques. At a temple in Jaipur, working Indian women convene in a swirl of saris during their lunch break to chat, listen to storytellers, and pray. I was disappointed to arrive too late; most of the women had left. However, the temple goddess did not fail to deliver a magical moment for me. Another late arrival prostrated herself on the patterned marble floor in front of the temple. She remained there long enough for me to compose this shot carefully with a 35–70mm zoom lens. *(left)* In Turkey, light falling on a tiled wall in a mosque provided a lyrical setting for a man at prayer. Sensitive to the surroundings, I worked quietly and quickly to get the moment on film with an 80–200mm zoom lens. *(above)*

THE WIDE-ANGLE approach to photojournalistic travel photography necessitates involvement in the subject. In southwestern France, along the Canal du Midi, I encountered a grandmother with her daughter and granddaughter. I knelt down to photograph the chubby baby from up close with a 24mm lens, but she would not raise her head. When the grandmother reached over to soothe the child, I was in the right place at the right time to snap the action, diapers and all. *(above)*

I MADE A photojournalistic portrait of a nation on the streets of Warsaw during Poland's political and economic rough period. A tired man selling tired flowers had fallen asleep. Rather than waking him up with a close-up, wide-angle approach, I reached for the 80–200mm zoom lens. With the grid screen in my viewfinder, I was easily able to keep the lines in the background plumb and square. *(right)*

SHOOT QUICK, SHOOT SMART! This is the motto for today's travel photojournalist. In bustling markets it has become harder to get candid shots of people. Someone is always tipping off your subjects about the photographer aiming at them from over yonder. At Guatemala's Solola market, I quickly shot a few frames of the Licuados fruit-drink stand. Then I got smart; I lowered the camera and looked else-where, waiting for people to leave the stand before the vendor was tipped off. The coast clear, I contin-ued shooting to record the pretty paint job in plain view. *(above)*

I GO FOR any photojournalistic situation that reveals a culture's identity. In San Miguel de Allende, Mexico, a delivery boy resting on a stack of Jesus paintings was a charming photo opportunity illustrat-ing the country's religious leanings. *(left)*

SHOOTING
SPECIAL
EVENTS

....

AS A ROOKIE STAFF PHOTOGRAPHER

on the *Boston Globe,* I was taught to cover the bases of a news story when

shooting a special event. This meant to capture three types of shots: overall,

medium, and close-up. The picture editor scrutinized my take on each assign-

ment to make sure I'd gotten this triptych. This gave him maximum leeway in

selecting a single shot with the most journalistic impact, or a sequential pic-

ture story of several images. Today, I take a variety of pictures to capture the

spirit of a special event or adventure in a personal, interpretive manner. Though

I'm not on assignment for a newsmagazine, I generally still try to cover the journalistic bases for a comprehensive picture story.

The classic triptych of images that I learned to take so long ago is still important when trying to capture a special event. The overall shot tends to be in the recording mode. It's the picture that conveys the activity in the context of its location. Often taken with a wide-angle lens, the overall shot is usually the weakest image in a picture story. While it is an important ingredient to a picture story, it is a generality, not a specific statement. For this reason, it often lacks visual impact or editorial point of view.

WHEN SHOOTING special events, I try to come up with a symbolic image that reflects the happening. To illustrate the annual Venice Winter Carnival, I combined two symbolic elements. Knowing that the Lion of Venice is the city's mascot, I festooned the statue with carnival streamers, carefully arranging the curlicues around the lion's mane. *(page 102)*

The medium shot, or story-flow picture, is a more specific statement of the event. Closer to the action, the medium shot aims to capture some of the human interaction of the experience. It can be taken with either a wide-angle or a telephoto lens. Regardless of the lens used, to be successful the medium shot should give the viewer a sense of being involved in the action.

The close-up shot is a symbolic detail. Generally an interpretive image, the close-up *implies*—it does not *describe*. Of the three types of images, the detail often has the least information and the most graphic impact. However, if only one picture can run in a newsmagazine or newspaper, the close-up seldom makes it; it's the medium shot that usually gets published. While graphic close-ups are constantly used in fashion, beauty, automotive, and other editorial and commercial fields, editors and art directors of newspapers and travel magazines usually think they are too minimal for reportorial use.

PHOTOJOURNALISTIC THINKING includes finding ways to have subjects all to yourself. To prevent tourists and other photographers from interfering with my photograph of a carnival harlequin, I asked him to pose on a narrow dock with the Santa Maria Maggiore church in the distance. Other shooters stuck on the quay waited in frustration, unable to walk on the water to ruin my picture. *(preceding page)*

I'm a believer in interpretive travel details, and to a certain extent, I've pioneered them in travel photography. To tell the whole story, however, I'll illustrate how I incorporated details into my total coverage of the Venice Winter Carnival. You will note, in fact, that I did not just take close-up shots; I followed the dictums of my old newspaper editor and covered all the bases.

IN RECORDING any special event I always take overall, medium, and close-up shots. I find, however, that most people do not go for the unusual detail images that can be so evocative of an experience. At the Carnival, I spotted a clump of *stelle filanti,* or carnival streamers, stuck in a classic Venetian wall. With the wind whipping the streamers horizontally, the sight was too weird to pass up. *(above)* I also made still-life images of my handmade leather carnival mask on some of the magnificent marble floors found in churches and palazzi around the city. *(left)*

WHEN I ENCOUNTERED Mrs. Moon and Mr. Sun, I was standing next to the famous Campanile, Venice's lookout tower. The base of the tower was made of Italian marble and presented a perfect background for a portrait of the couple. The subtle coloration of their costumes against the gray and pink stone added to the sophistication of the image. *(above)*

ATTENDING LA FENICE, Venice's opera house, is a must for carnival shooters. People dressed flamboyantly hang out of gilded boxes, attracting attention to themselves. So as not to attract attention to myself, I brown-bagged my camera going in and shot unobtrusively with a handheld camera before the performance and during intermission. I used daylight-balanced, high-speed film, which gave the tungsten-lit interior a warm tone. *(opposite top)*

TO COVER special events, I carry, at the very least, a 20–35mm wide-angle zoom lens, a 60mm or 100mm macro lens, and an 80–200mm zoom lens. I used the full lens range at the Venice Winter Carnival. The wide-angle zoom captured the spontaneity of these revelers under the Campanile. *(opposite bottom)*

TAKING PLACE in February the week before Lent, the Venice Winter Carnival attracts participants from throughout Europe. Dressed as harlequins, punchinellos, Dantes, Cleopatras, and a wide variety of really tacky clowns with red balls on their noses, these characters love having their pictures taken. Although I prefer the more classical commedia dell'arte costumes, such as the punchinello with the Church of the Salute beyond *(above)*, I also took advantage of all the glitz on three trips to the Carnival. In the photograph on the opposite page, I used a color-coordinated wall as a background for this couple in neon netting.

SEEING COLOR, FORM, AND CONTENT

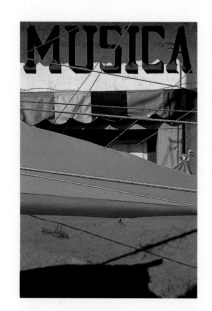

·······································

AS A CHILD I ADORED MY DELUXE box of Crayolas—I loved *looking* at the crayons as much as using them. I stared endlessly at the crayon log cabins I constructed in my bedroom, kaleidoscopic creations with roofs made out of colorful craft paper. Eventually I graduated from Crayolas to Japanese watercolors, and again I would stare at the graduated colors in the beautiful wood box. However, not until I was exposed to the exuberant palette of third-world countries did my love of color really explode. For me, as a travel photographer, color is no longer contained in little squares in a paint box—it is all over the map. I can now love color around the world in all its permutations. I'm enamored of the vibrant colors of northern India just as much as I like the soothing earth hues of Ireland. Before I see light, form, texture, or even subject—I see color. Color is, indeed, the primary content of many of my photographs.

The basis of all formal art training for a painter is learning how to work within the framework of the gray scale by executing pencil or charcoal drawing of still lifes and the human figure. Only after this exercise is the student allowed to introduce color. Similarly, having black-and-white literacy is fundamental to successful color photography. Learning how to conceptualize in monochrome is a prerequisite to developing an effective color vision.

THE FORM OF a photograph is based on how the visual elements are organized in a composition irrespective of color, while volume is how color occupies space as a quality, giving the illusion of three dimensions. Light and dark values, or highlight and shadow areas, provide the "push-pull" in any formal treatment of color. The dark values pull the eye in, the light values push the eye away. Together they create visual tension. Both the photograph of Indian marigolds in a bag *(page 110)* and that of a Mexican *musica* sign in a market *(preceding page)* are more about the formal issues of form, value, and volume than they are about their literal subjects.

Robert Hughes made an interesting observation in his book *The Shock of the New,* a compilation of his BBC television series. Referring to the nineteenth century, he stated: "Every educated person drew as a matter of course. . . . Drawing was an ordinary form of speech, used as a pastime or aide-memoire, without pretensions to 'high' art. Nevertheless, this general graphic literacy was the compost from which the great depictive artists of the late nineteenth and early twentieth centuries were able to grow: Degas, Eakins, Picasso, Matisse. It was gradually abolished by the mass camera market."

Today, this "general graphic literacy" is in fact a general photographic literacy. Everyone now "draws" with a camera. However, those aspiring to rise from the photographic compost must first learn to "draw" with black-and-white film. I find that people who have worked with black-and-white film tend to have a better compositional sense in color. They take fewer color-for-color's-sake pictures, in which color is used as a crutch rather than as a treatment. But because many color photographers have not learned to deal with form and content in black and white, color is not intelligently or intuitively integrated in their work. In monochrome, a photograph must convey a message without the sensual distraction of color—the image must have enough content to get the message across to the viewer. Furthermore, the photograph must have effective form—it must be well composed and visually succinct to elucidate the content. Black and white is primarily cerebral, while color is essentially visceral.

Richard Whelan writes in *Double Take:* "When we look at a color photograph, we see, first and foremost, colors and their interrelationships. When we look at black-and-white photographs, we see, first and foremost, forms and their interrelationships." By eliminating color, which demands so much attention, we can grasp the content and appreciate the form of an image much more easily. It is only through trial and error that we learn to make photographs that are balanced, that are as intelligent as they are sensual.

Until quite recently, many photographic artists and critics maintained that color photography was inferior to black-and-white. This was because few practitioners of color had managed to get beyond using color as a crutch. As Sally Euclaire recounts in her book *The New Color Photography:* "Walker Evans deemed color a vulgar medium and stated that many color photographers confuse color with noise and that they blow you down with screeching hues alone . . . a bebop of electric hues, furious reds, and poisonous greens." There is no denying that there has been a promiscuous use of color in photography. For the photographer, the big challenge is to control color. And when color and content are as deeply intermeshed as they are in travel photography, there is a double challenge.

COLOR HARMONY is the compound effect of two or more colors and how they play off each other. In the real world of take-it-or-leave-it color, the travel photographer achieves color harmony by perceiving compatible color relationships and by carefully orchestrating them in the viewfinder. In Old Nice, under a fruit vendor's stall, I saw these cast-off tomatoes and some typical French purple and green wrapping paper. Much to the vendor's amusement, I was down on the ground orchestrating a color-intensive image of his garbage.

Unlike creative people working in other media the photographer is not in complete control of his or her color destiny; he or she must accept the alchemy dished out by reality and chemistry. (Computer technology may soon change this: the ability to fine-tune chromas on the electronic screen will probably give photographers even more control over color than painters now have.) Color can certainly be at its most garish, flippant, and fun in travel photography. Yet so many travel pictures seem, unfortunately, to be reflex responses to color stimulus. "Isn't that a colorful sight?" the tourist exclaims—then he immediately snaps at it, producing what R. P. Kingston calls "neat little windows that look through onto perfectly believable rectangles of colored commonplace."

To avoid the common color pitfalls, strive to develop a treatment of color that reveals as much about your own style as do your treatments of form and content. If you can resolve the garish, common world of color into provocative images in which chroma, form, and content strike a balance, then you can throw away the color crutch.

WHILE COLOR photography has gained increasing acceptance in recent years, the travel photographer still has a challenge dealing with the global rise of garish, chemical colors. The neon-colored gloves of these Japanese schoolboys were grounded by the boys' black uniforms. The result is a surreal shot of Day-Glo color. *(opposite top)*

"IS COLOR CONTENT?" has been a long-debated question within the art establishment. In certain fields of the photographic medium, color-for-color's-sake imagery is still the kiss of death; it's an especially big pitfall for travel photographers. For me, the degree to which color is information is the degree to which color is content. In a close-up of the uniform worn by a Queen's Guard in London, the red of his coat is not gratuitous, it is informational. *(opposite bottom)*

I AM OFTEN asked how I get so much color in my travel photographs. I actually see the chromatic qualities of subjects before I recognize subject matter. By underexposing slide film and saturating the hues, I squeeze as much concentrated color onto film as possible. Saturation, or intensity, is the degree of purity of a color relative to the three undiluted primary colors: yellow, red, and blue. My photograph of velvet Navajo skirts for sale at Santa Fe's annual Indian market is a study in color concentration and saturation. *(above)*

ALL THE WORLD is a canvas, so introduce your own color! The pink doorway in Ecuador was nice but not a picture. Thinking that my rental car would add the necessary element of color, I drove it into my preconceived picture. I framed the shot with a 20mm lens from a low angle to incorporate the car and the door. Suddenly, a woman wearing a red sweater appeared at the doorway. I got more color than I had bargained for. *(opposite top)*

WHEN I'M shooting in an exotic country market, I'm often disappointed by how hard it is to find clean, colorful shots uncompromised by white styrofoam cups, plastic bags, and just plain garbage. Whenever possible, I take this stuff out of the picture before shooting. In a Guatemalan market, I was delighted to find a pristine color image in these watermelon sections for sale, complete with a colorful, corrugated background. *(right)*

IMAGINE HOW flat the New Mexican windows *(above)* would be at historic Las Golondrinas without the bits of red geranium popping out the window for light and air. Just a spot of color made all the difference. However, at times a totally monochromatic photo can stand no improvement from the introduction of color. On a trek in Nepal, the quality of light on some water pots provided a lovely, monochromatic image. *(opposite)*

LOCAL COLOR may not be revealed in the invasive values of clashing chromas. It may be found in such authentic compositions as this bull hood ornament on a Mexican truck. The combination of the silver bull, the gray wrought-iron railing, and the red vehicle makes a sophisticated cultural statement. *(above)* Equally authentic are the subtle colors of the designs in a nomad's tent. Woven from camel and goat hair, these Moroccan shepherds' tents are color coordinated with the North African landscape. *(left)*

COLOR IMPACT is achieved through strategic lens use. I augmented the chromatic impact of these Mexican brooms by using a 24mm lens and angling along the colored wall to lead the eye up to the brooms. *(above)* In a Mexican market, hatbands streaming from a stack of straw hats for sale suggested a different optical strategy. I used a 60mm macro lens to move in, filling the frame edge-to-edge with the colorful hatbands. *(right)*

LIGHT,
PATTERN, AND
TEXTURE

....

I AM FREQUENTLY ASKED WHETHER I hang up my cameras at midday, only shooting during the prime time of dawn and dusk. The answer is: I'll shoot anytime, as long as there's light. Regardless of the time of day, it's light that enhances pattern and dimensionality and augments color and texture in the photographable world.

Through the dramatic organization of light and shadow, travel photographers can achieve a high level of interpretation and abstraction in all their subjects. There are, however, technical challenges in dealing with light.

SEEING THE perfect light is easy when it's abstract and creating definitive highlight and shadow areas. For example, a courtyard in India provided a clean, canvaslike surface for the play of abstract light. *(page 122)* Picturesque illumination is obvious in nighttime Paris, the City of Lights. At dusk, great shots can be made of the Eiffel Tower that include nearby buildings with illuminated windows. *(preceding page)*

How film records light is one important consideration. To ensure optimum highlight and shadow detail on slide film, most professional photographers routinely bracket their exposures. Bracketing is not necessary for print film, given its greater exposure latitudes. Bracketing is achieved by taking the exposure your camera's meter indicates. Then you take two other exposures, one a stop over the metered exposure, the other a stop under. Most modern cameras have an automatic bracketing mode, making this process very easy. I bracket in full-stop increments when the contrast level in the subject is high, and at half-stop increments in flat light. When in doubt, which is often, I bracket both ways.

LIGHT PERCEIVED to be imperfect is often avoided by photographers due to fears regarding the proper exposure. I use my in-camera spot meter when dealing with dramatic backlit and side-lit situations, like the row of guards at London's Queen's Day Parade. *(opposite top)* Strong images can also be made in flat, stormy light. At New Mexico's Las Golondrinas, I underexposed to create a silhouette of the graveyard cross and *morada. (opposite bottom)*

I'm also often in doubt about how weather is going to affect my travel photographs. In overcast conditions, when pattern and texture are subtler, I find I have to be extra careful in organizing my compositions. When the sun breaks through the clouds, pattern and texture come alive. And if a distinct pattern or texture is enhanced by raking light, I really have something to hang my camera on. Patterned or textured surfaces, whether man-made or natural, promise almost perfect compositions; all I have to do is frame them through the viewfinder. Light, pattern, and texture then converge to create images I can reach into with my eyes and almost feel, a kind of visual braille.

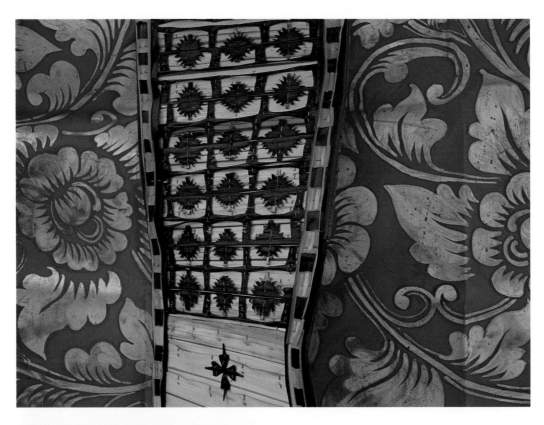

PATTERN, OR THE disposition of elements in a subject, is a great visual hook to hang a composition on. In fact, pattern can almost become the composition. All you have to do is give it boundaries through the viewfinder. The third world offers kaleidoscopic patterns with abandon: stripes with checks and dots, plaids with florals, and more. At an Indonesian temple, I framed up a detail of the fabric and straw woven band decorating a shrine to creates a study in pattern and change of scale *(above),* while in North Yemen, a painted door induced a formal composition that plays off volumes of color with pattern *(left).*

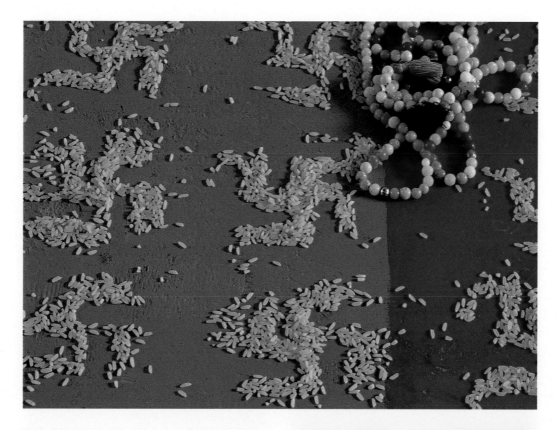

THE QUALITY OF texture contributes to creating
a sense of three dimensions on two-dimensional film,
and provides a feeling-of-place in destination photography. Not necessarily confined to shots of ancient,
distressed walls and wrinkled faces, texture was present in an Indian temple where I recorded rice
arranged in curious swastika shapes. *(above)* Texture
also animates a picture of handmade brooms in the
Caribbean. *(right)* Although light enhances textural
subjects, both these images were taken in flat light;
they still retain their feeling-of-place.

APPRECIATING ABSTRACTS, MYSTERIES, AND GRAPHICS

· ·

P HOTOGRAPHERS FREQUENTLY BECOME

known for signature characteristics in their images. In my case, I've developed an eye for graphic details from the travel environment. This vision evolved over the years from my awareness that the generic, overall travel shot was becoming harder and harder to come by. Traditional travel images were increasingly compromised by such elements as cars, parking lots, telephone wires, signs, and a myriad of unwanted, contemporary distractions. The more I stepped back to get in the whole scene, the more vulnerable I was to including these elements. The farther in I moved, the more control I had over the subject. Moving in closer and closer to my subjects thus became a problem-solving device long before I began to nurture this vision into a signature style. Further influencing me to optical intimacy with my subjects was photojournalist Robert Capa's statement, "If your pictures aren't strong enough, you're not close enough."

WE DO NOT ALWAYS have to convey recognizable subject matter in our destination imagery. I think effective imagery, born of the imagination, should take the viewer from fact to feeling. Abstract images are those in which the literal subject is obscure or completely unidentifiable; transcending subject matter is thus the key to abstraction. In travel photography, it's hard to totally eliminate subject matter—nor is it always desirable in a field that is grounded in conveying information. The best we can do most of the time is to approach abstraction, as I did with the beaded strands crossing the back of a Samburu dancer in Kenya. *(page 128)* Similarly, a peephole in the torn fabric of a maharaja's palanquin in the Jodhpur Museum is both abstract and mysterious. *(preceding page)*

As I moved in closer on subjects, an abstract quality developed in my work. In the fine arts, an abstract painting is nonrepresentational. The treatment dominates the subject matter to the point where the literal subject is either obscure or absolutely indecipherable. In abstract works of art, representing reality is *not* the artist's intent.

The word *abstract* is often used loosely in connection with photography. In straight or unmanipulated photography there is no such thing as true abstraction. Even racked down to its closest focus or greatest magnification, the camera's lens is recording reality—you would have to throw the lens totally out of focus to render a subject truly abstract. As Elliot Porter said, "In the painterly sense, there isn't anything really abstract about a photograph made with a lens, because it's not entirely a product of the photographer's imagination. . . . The subject is usually a detail of something."

The best you can do with unmanipulated photography is to *approach* abstraction. And why is approaching abstraction desirable in travel photography? By moving in close on the graphic details of the world, I find that the resulting quality of seeming abstraction adds a formal compositional rigor and a mystery to my images. What we leave out of a composition is far more important than what we decide to include. If we include too much, the essential subject is weakened—we lose the aesthetic tension of the composition and dilute the mystery.

Diane Arbus once said, "A picture should be a mystery about a mystery. The more it tells you, the less you know." The quality of mystery is as important in a photographic image as it is in a human being. To hold something back, not to be an open book, is considered an attractive quality in a person. The same holds true for a photograph. The part that implies the whole invites the viewer's intellectual interaction and stimulates the imagination much more than does the see-Spot-run picture. Images that strive to tell it

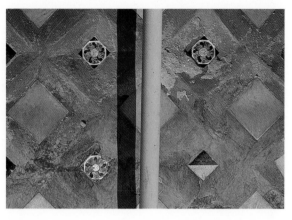

all actually discourage sustained viewing. I find in travel magazines they serve as fillers.

Travel photographs that stop you in your tracks, on the other hand, have a lot to declare. These are images captured at the confluence of mystery, light, graphics, and abstraction. And you don't have to be a professional to be the beneficiary of the rare instances when these qualities consort for your camera—I've seen many "stoppers" at my workshops from amateur photographers. How can it happen for you? The answer comes in the form of a Buddhist proverb: Chance (opportunity) comes to the prepared mind.

Photographic guru Minor White was a student of Eastern philosophies and a great believer in the personal benefits of seeking abstraction in photography. In *Rites and Passages*, he wrote: "The camera is a means of self-discovery and of

ABSTRACTION OFTEN results from the formal aesthetic treatment of nominal subjects. Artist-photographer Jan Groover got rave reviews in the late 1970s for her downtown New York City street scenes. Trucks and all, they were intersected by telephone poles and signposts. In my case, why not a shot of a yellow pole in Mexico with a sense-of-place tiled wall in back of it? If a gallery-represented photographer had shot this ten or fifteen years ago, it might have hung in a show. If I submitted it to a travel magazine today, the art director would think I'd gotten too abstract.

growth. If that self is not large, or intense, one need not give up art. The camera and the technique of abstraction will broaden one, deepen one immeasurably."

To delve deeper into the mysteries of travel photography, learn to go beyond strictly optical relationships with your subjects. You must look closer in order to see deeper. This practice causes the world to yield up its discreet detail images for you. Like panning for gold in a rushing stream, good photographs aren't just lying on the surface waiting to be scooped up. In today's travel environment, awash with modernity and homogeneity, we have to pan more deeply for creative images.

Another word that is loosely used in connection with photography is *graphic. Graphic* means that the work—whether it be literature or one of the arts—describes clearly, depicts vividly, and is easily deciphered by the reader or viewer. *Graphic* is usually considered to be synonymous with impact in photography—and impact certainly is a virtue in travel photography. The truth is that every photograph you take is graphic by definition. The camera as a recording device takes a clear, descriptive image of reality every time the shutter is released. So what you are striving for is the visual impact that derives from a highly refined optical approach to subjects in which the alchemy of abstracts, mysteries, and graphics sustains prolonged viewing.

"GRAPHIC" IS A THROWAWAY word of the visual arts: it means to depict something in realistic and vivid detail. The exotic world is replete with the raw material for graphic photographs, and the search for the inherently graphic has been the Holy Grail of my destination photography. Exotic third world countries make the search easy for me with their ubiquitous painted surfaces. For example, the pyramidal painted wall behind stacks of Indonesian rice bundles was a natural. *(opposite top)* More exotic imagery was found in Morocco on an orange shipping crate, where the indigo symbol lent a graphic quality to the picture. Had the crates been plain, I wouldn't have taken the shot. *(opposite bottom)*

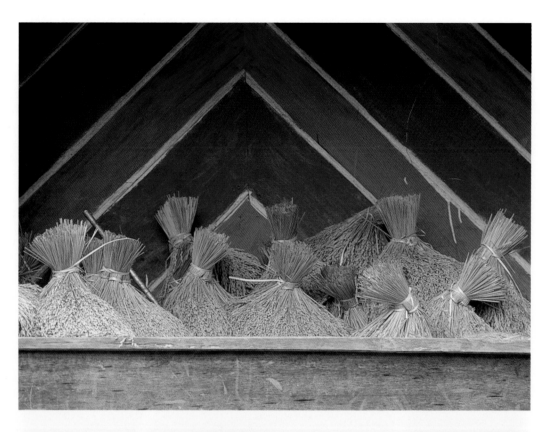

GRAPHIC QUALITIES are not endemic to exotic countries only. Apple-pie America has its graphic moments too, especially when shadows play across its classical New England architecture. *(left and above)* Light is mysterious ephemera, constantly revealing secrets about the surfaces it moves across.

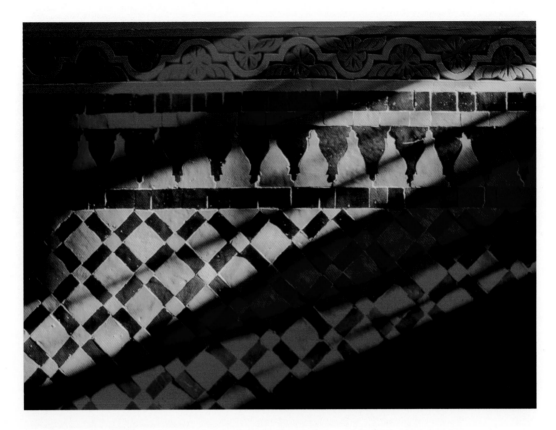

CAPTURING GLIMPSES of mystery in the travel environment is a tricky business. You really have to be in the local groove to feel mystery and you have to be a spirit photographer to capture it before the quality disappears into thin air. I was sunbathing on a Mexican beach when a rug vendor stared down at me from behind his product. Squinting and about to shoo him off, I snapped to attention photographically to record the beachcombing presence. *(opposite)* At the Palais Jamai Hotel in Fez, Morocco, I was stopped by the extraordinary light streaming through a stained-glass window onto a Moroccan tiled wall. I shot it immediately; mysterious light doesn't hang around. *(above)*

THE ART
OF THE
LANDSCAPE

∙∙∙

Landscapes will always hold
the greatest attraction for travel photographers. Although the global environment struggles desperately with the multiple threats of toxic waste, ambient
garbage, and commercial and touristic development, people can discover in
landscape photographs the ineffable spirit, awesome majesty, and enduring
style of nature. Mankind maintains a connection with the earth—the more
sublime the terrain, the more resonant the relationship. And landscape photographs are symbols of this relationship; they reflect the photographer's

yearning to be in harmony with a natural order.

This emotional attraction can become a pitfall to many amateur travel photographers. With practically every pretty view, out comes the camera. Landscape pictures are taken without the kind of value judgment commonly brought to bear on other subjects. The tendency seems to be that an emotional response to a landscape means it is worth the film. When these travelers get back home and view the results, they remember the emotional response, but are disappointed by how the scene translated onto film.

CONSIDERING A silhouette shot of a goat tethered to a tree on a beach in Martinique, I noticed a girl striding down the sand. The camera was already set up on a tripod for an evening seascape, which I snapped when the girl crossed the viewfinder. *(page 138)*

This common disappointment with landscape photographs is a by-product of various miscalculations. Yes, many landscapes are indeed pretty to the naked eye, but you must always stop to ask yourself, will this landscape hold up on film?

Three-dimensional reality rendered on two-dimensional film often falls short of our creative aspirations. With landscapes, consider whether enough dimensionality is created by light, texture, or color to stand up on a two-dimensional surface. This question must, of course, be asked regardless of the subject matter. But because landscapes are generally more distant from the camera than other subjects, they are more vulnerable to flatness or loss of dimensionality.

MOST AVID landscape photographers are also mad about nature studies. Although I nearly went mad from the heat and blisters I endured hiking into the Haleakala Crater on Maui, I got a sharp-edged, surreal nature study of the silver sword-plant with a 60mm macro lens. Nature images can always be improved by moving in as close as possible on them. *(preceding page)*

The professional landscape photographer is generally sensitive to the sharpness and contrast of both his lenses and the film he uses. Again, because the landscape is often over "yonder," image quality and detail become all-important. More demands are placed on optics and emulsions in landscape photography, since they must stand up to ultraviolet light, haze, dust, extreme temperatures, and foul weather.

If you do a lot of landscape photography, you will want to consider the optical quality of the lens system you use and to experiment with different films to determine which emulsion best interprets your style. Don't necessarily opt for the sharpest film on the market, either. Your style may be best served by a grainy film treatment.

Optical falloff is a major factor in landscape photography. Wide-angle lenses distort and spread visual elements across the film plane. When the camera is close to a subject, the exaggerated size of near elements is the result of optical distortion. In contrast, when the subject is remote, optical falloff comes into effect. That majestic mountain range you aimed a wide-angle lens at looks like foothills on film.

Don't use wide-angle lenses on landscapes just to "get it all in." In landscape photography, as in other fields, the part that implies the whole is often much more graphically dramatic than the entire mountain range. Switch to a telephoto lens and isolate the element of a scene that speaks to you the most clearly. It might not even be the highest peak that elicits the greatest visual and emotional response. The play of light, texture, pattern, and color might come together gloriously in the bottom of the valley. Don't allow yourself to be programmed for the obvious—the most common view is usually the touristic "photo opportunity" stop.

SUNSETS DON'T grab me photograpically: I'd rather watch them sitting with my feet up and a drink in hand. However, on a safari in Kenya I roused myself to snap this sunset. To make things easy, I placed the sun smack-dab in the middle, and I must say that I like the results. When exposing for sunsets, spot-meter off the sky and bracket the exposures to have a choice of exposures.

I use a wide-angle lens on a landscape when I want to include a foreground element in a scenic picture. If a landscape is not dramatic enough to stand up on its own, I'll search out or introduce a foreground element to provide both interest and dimensionality. This device takes the weight of visual responsibility off the weaker background scene. I don't allow the inclusion of foreground elements to become a facile formula, however. In my workshop, I've seen too many wretched trees inserted into mediocre landscape shots taken in national parks. I'm not saying to never include a tree or a branch—just make sure it has some aesthetic virtue and contributes graphically to the composition. Another dated cliché I still see is the inclusion of the "little woman" in a red jacket sitting, for color and scale, on a ledge overlooking the Grand Canyon.

As a creative tip toward transcending these clichés, consider this passage from Galen Rowell's *Mountain Light:* "I appreciate photographs not so much for the ways they precisely render reality as for the ways in which they transcend it. . . . When we are deeply moved by a photograph of a landscape, we are usually reacting to what I call the 'selective vision' of the photographer rather than to the fidelity of the scene itself."

But if the truth be told, while I adore scenery the world over, landscapes hold the least allure for me photographically. I dislike having no control whatsoever over the distant view. My own photographic style has much to do with the high level of control I exert over my subjects and shooting environments.

Landscape and mountaineering photographers, however, would probably disagree with my assessment that landscapes do not allow for hands-on involvement. For them, the challenge of having climbed the mountain, rappelled over the cliff, or walked on the water to get the shot is a heroic "body-on" experience. The physical demands and the magic of being in the right place at the right time are part of what fuels their creativity. For these photographers, the thought of leaving the cameras at base camp is a worse condition than altitude sickness.

Ansel Adams felt that great landscape photographs occur when "the realities of the external event pass through the eye-mind-spirit of the photographer" and are "transformed into interpretation and expression." What you like to photograph, how you treat your subjects aesthetically, and the lengths to which you will go to get your images will be factors as diverse as the mountains, valleys, seas, and skies that make up our environment.

I UNDERSTAND why Georgia O'Keeffe didn't like being at Lake George with Stieglitz. "Too much green; what am I to paint?" O'Keeffe complained. Many overgreen landscape shots lack interesting light, texture, and compositional rigor. There are exceptions, though. Even in flat light, this verdant Indonesian scene is enhanced by the textural changes in the green, brushy trees and the tiny shrines. *(opposite top)*

ABOUT AS SIMPLE as it gets, this shot of Morocco's High Atlas Mountains behind a palm tree was easy to miss. Using a tripod and an 80–200mm zoom lens, I stopped down the lens to f22 to get the maximum depth-of-field. To avoid camera motion when using a tripod for telephoto landscape shots, make sure the center column, legs, and knobs are all tightly adjusted. *(opposite bottom)*

REINVENTING LANDSCAPE photography takes a little imagination, such as the time I saw a friend's Appaloosa horse, an Indian breed, grazing with Black Mesa in the distance. Black Mesa is a sacred site to the Native Americans living in the San Ildefonso pueblo in northern New Mexico. I put the two elements together in a symbolic landscape. *(left)*

ABSTRACTION IN outdoor photography is hard to come by, since landscapes prefer having pretty, descriptive pictures made of them. This photograph is fairly abstract, with its cut tulip heads lying in rows between the beds. In general, abstraction in land-scape photography usually works best with a narrow-er optical point of view. *(above)*

LAYERED MIST, mountains, clouds, haze, and land often create pleasing landscape photographs. Such layering adds an abstract quality to high-altitude photographs such as this one taken in Nepal. *(above)* The normal instinct is to shoot most landscapes in a horizontal format. Our peripheral orientation likes to get it all in—the whole damn mountain range. In Canyonlands, Utah, however, the leading line created by the shadow dictated a vertical format for this scene I came upon during an Outward Bound program. *(left)*

THE EYE GOES to the lightest point in any picture. An empty sky drags the eye up and out of the photograph. Crop it out, I say. On a typical English day in the Cotswolds, I lowered the camera down onto the autumnal ground to minimize the whiteout sky. *(opposite)*

LANDMARK CHALLENGES

....

ALTHOUGH THEY WOULD SEEM TO
be the easiest subjects in the roster of travel themes, landmarks can, in fact,
be disappointing photo opportunities. Today, historic cathedrals, buildings, and
monuments are often surrounded by unscenic parking lots loaded with buses,
with flocks of tour groups fluttering around their entrances. Over the years I've
found some aesthetic devices to overcome these modern elements; some of my
treatments even include the cars and buses to graphic effect. If I can't fight it,
I join it!

You can always eliminate unwanted elements by moving in close with a wide-angle lens and angling up on a landmark. Similarly you can shoot only a detail of it. But there are new views on the world's architectural heritage. These

fresh angles and novel interpretations require a little imagination; you must be willing to investigate unorthodox angles and combinations of elements around a landmark. For example, you can use wide-angle techniques and incorporate graphically effective distortion into landmark images, or use telephoto compression to achieve unexpected relationships.

AN EFFECTIVE way to handle photographs of landmarks is to frame them with a strong foreground element. On one of my photo tours to India, members of my group wanted models at the Taj Mahal for early-morning shots. Two people agreed to pose and bought saris in the hotel shop. When I saw their selection, I was concerned about the lack of color in the saris. On film, however, the black and gray saris really worked, allowing the landmark to read well in the warm morning light. *(page 148)* At London's Big Ben, a tough landmark customer, I framed the tower with another tough customer—a statue of Winston Churchill provided the needed element. *(preceding page)* While at Indonesia's Borobudur temple, I placed a temple spire between conical crenellations on an opposite wall. *(above)*

I enjoy including people in a landmark picture, such as interesting locals or amusing tourists. But make sure these passersby are a genuine contribution to the editorial or artistic content of the image. As in landscapes, the old-fashioned approach is to include people to give scale or color; this technique will render clichéd landmark pictures.

When you have the opportunity to work a landmark photographically from many angles, make sure to allocate sufficient time to do so. The Eiffel Tower, Bangkok's temples, Big Ben, the Taj Mahal, Indonesia's Borobudur temple—these places are great to hit in the early morning or evening when the tour buses are at a minimum or are gone. Using a variety of lenses and angles, you'll enjoy spending time, knowing you'll come away with a comprehensive coverage of these great landmarks.

Above all, as a travel photographer, remember that you don't need to take a strictly architectural approach to landmarks. Unless you actually want a straight recording shot of a building as an academic reference, you should strive to transcend the traditional postcard approach to shooting landmarks.

WHAT ABOUT PLACING the "little woman" in
landmark shots just for scale and color? I do it all the
time, except it's my husband, Landt, who poses for
me. He unexpectedly came into the picture at Castle
Howard, where Evelyn Waugh's *Brideshead Revisited*
was filmed. On a misty, winter morning with the
water frozen over in the fountains, he was waiting
patiently for me to finish photographing. As I walked
up to him sitting on the edge of a fountain, I saw the
potential for this image—a fashionable landmark
shot. Yes, Landt really dresses this way when he's not
in jeans. *(above)* Finding details of Paris's Notre
Dame Cathedral too dull, I asked Landt to pose again,
this time wearing a beret for a Magritte-like shot of
the rose window. *(right)*

PARKED CARS WERE a problem when photographing Rome's Arch of Constantine. Discovering the arch reflected in a windshield, I was inspired to incorporate the reflection and the surrounding vehicles into a wide-angle composition. This image, with its neutral colors and moody sky, worked well enough to win first place in a photo contest. *(above)* Another photographic challenge in major cities today is the tour groups swarming around every landmark. At St. Peter's Square in Rome the piazza was buzzing with tourists. I retreated to the far end of the square, where I found a horse carriage. The red wheel was perfect for superimposing over the piazza, and during a lull in the crowds, a Bible-toting priest walked into the picture. *(left)*

SEARCHING FOR fresh angles on landmarks is like a photographic treasure hunt. On the prowl at Bangkok's Grand Palace, I discovered a composition that reflects the exotic atmosphere of the place; it is layered, intricate, mysterious, multifaceted, and textured. *(above)* On another photographic treasure hunt in Belgium, I wandered up a flight of restaurant stairs in Brussels to check out the Grand Place below. A flag filled with wind was the surprise discovery and became a graphic foreground element for this shot of a spire. *(right)*

MOST LANDMARKS are monochromatic, and they come off a dull gray or brown on film. Looking for a good angle on the Chrysler Building, I saw American flags hanging in front of the New York Daily News Building. The flags reflected needed color in the building's plate glass, with the Chrysler Building doubling up as well. *(above)* Similarly, striving to introduce color into a photograph of London's Big Ben, I found a classic English phonebox to incorporate into the shot. *(left)* At Tikal, Guatemala's Mayan temple complex, I caught cultural color on a wild shirt. I shot the man from the back, with a temple rising behind him to maximize the impact of the patterned shirt, and I asked him to turn his head so I could also catch his profile. *(opposite)*

INTERPRETING THE TRAVEL EXPERIENCE

....

I OFTEN USE THE WORD "INTERPRETIVE"

in connection with travel photographs. I'm referring here to a type of image that reflects the photographer's personal and creative relationship with a foreign culture. An interpretive travel image has little in common with a recording approach to destination photography. The intent is to do more than create "a sense of place," as wonderful as that may be. It is to imaginatively recreate "a feel of place" on film. Interpretive travel images capture the photographer's feelings about a place, while at the same time they reflect formal aesthetic concerns. Conveying the facts or offering a literal and descriptive likeness of the subject is not the goal.

The surface facts of the world are, after all, known to most educated people: the Alps are rugged; the Eiffel Tower is tall; the Pyramids are triangular; the Great Wall of China is winding. Thousands of pictures have told us so—even if we have never seen these sights with our own eyes, we're saturated by their reality. D. H. Lawrence writes in *The Spell of New Mexico:* "Superficially, the world has become small and known. Poor little globe of earth, the tourists trot round you as easily as they trot round the Bois or round Central Park. There is no mystery left, we've been there, we've seen it, we know all about it. We've done the globe."

Lawrence made this pathetic point in the 1920s. If he were alive today, he would most likely agree with art critic John Russell, who counsels that only by a profound rethinking of our intellectual intent and aesthetic and creative treatment will today's artists be able to transcend the reality of an overexposed globe. This is a great challenge for artists working in every medium, including travel photographers, both amateur and professional.

WHY SHOULD THE travel photographer be limited by fixed reality? It's not even an issue for the painter or sculptor, who is usually interpreting reality rather than recording it. To arrive at more interpretive travel imagery, I frequently move elements. At a gas station in Kenya, for instance, I got my best wildlife shot by rearranging some Masai necklaces for sale against the batik giraffes. *(page 156)* At a temple in Thailand, I placed a monk's black water pot on a fence surrounded by saffron robes hanging out to dry. *(preceding page)*

In a brilliant *New York Times* essay titled "How Art Makes Us Feel at Home in the World," Russell speaks highly of photography's promise as a conveyor of a sense of place: "Photography in particular seemed to have everything in its favor. It was instantaneous. You could do it anywhere. In its early days it had an element of surprise, and almost the supernatural, that painting had long lost. It didn't take half a lifetime to learn, and it was a democratic art, one in which all began as equals. . . . It was in photography, if anywhere, that a sense of place would henceforth find its home."

Because it is such a democratic medium, photography is within the technical reach of millions, but it remains largely beyond their aesthetic grasp. Because using a camera can be such an instantaneous act, even serious photographers can get away with investing little time in creative thinking. I've had painters join some of my foreign photo trips. They just barely get a scene sketched in while the photographers have shot six pictures. In the rush, the elusive element of creative connectedness all too often escapes the photographer's lens.

John Russell amplifies on the challenge: "But now we have the Andes in the image bank, along with just about every other place in the gazetteer. . . . On the level of literal acquaintance and documentary charting we have a degree of orientation . . . but on the level of imaginative re-creation? That is another matter. . . . For seeing is not knowing, and where there is no imaginative re-creation we respond momentarily or not at all."

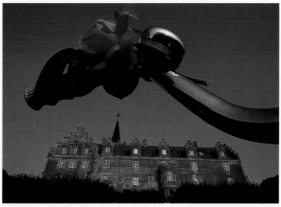

Have you ever asked yourself why your travel photographs don't seem to hold up to thoughtful viewing or why they don't sustain prolonged appreciation? I ask these questions about my own work on a regular basis. If your pictures seem to be all surface, with little or no depth, it's probably time to "internalize" being a travel photographer. You can embark on this personal and aesthetic journey by paying close attention to your feelings and reactions to a place, especially during the first days after arrival when your senses are being stimulated and challenged the most.

ONE OF MY first attempts at the creative interpretation of travel photography came on an assignment to photograph a bicycle trip through Denmark. Cycling alone but needing to create the sense of a group experience, I was at a loss for a line of cyclists cruising through the countryside. At Tranaeker Castle on the island of Langeland, I solved the problem by utilizing my handlebar with a color-coordinated rose. I dramatized the effect with a 20mm lens.

Think about the essence of the destination on an intellectual level. Surreal art photographer Duane Michals said, "Photography to me is a matter of thinking rather than looking. It's revelation, not description." It is also important to be in touch with your visceral reactions to a foreign culture. As both the visceral and cerebral impressions affect you, the foreign environment takes on new light, form, color, and texture. The environment offers images for your consideration that you never dreamed possible. Don't scuttle your receptivity to this new subject matter with too much critical judgment as to whether it will render a great travel photograph. Give in to the attraction. You can analyze the validity of the image later. Only in this way will you learn what works and where you are being led creatively. New camera angles will occur to you as you consider how to treat an unorthodox subject. You aren't just recording; you are interpreting a sense of place. And while you're at it, you may be expanding the definition of travel photography.

Surrender yourself to this process. Stop wondering about how your pictures will turn out. The picture taking will take on a new energy, I promise. Your vision will no longer be governed by programmed notions of what and how you should photograph on a trip—or even whether it's travel photography. The only thing that will matter is expression, pulling out all the stops on imaginative re-creation.

IMAGINATIVE INTERPRETATION comes into play when we allow ourselves to be visually playful. In Hawaii, I bought a "tee-lei" for my golfing father-in-law and threw it in the back of the car. Coming upon a golf course in dramatic, stormy light, I decided to photograph the tee-lei lying in a sandpit. I suddenly had a better idea when I saw Landt bringing the lei to me, wearing it around his neck. I played a different game, resulting in a funny, surreal reinterpretation of golf, Hawaiian style.

It's important to recognize that style isn't the issue here. What you are striving for is vision. In this process, any ongoing style loses its self-consciousness. Don't try to force an old style into a new vision, or vice versa. As Edward T. Hall puts it, "Vision in photography differs from style as depth does from surface. Style can only submit to vision."

As I allowed myself to be seduced by uncommon attractions in my travel photography, my own graphic style emerged. Whether my style serves vision and subject—or the other way around—is an ongoing question to me. But I know that style must always go beyond mere gesture to become a metaphor for an interpretive sense of place.

You may wonder what happens to traditional travel subjects and themes with interpretation and imaginative re-creation. Well, they don't disappear off the face of the earth, I assure you. My travel photographs are all *of* something. But they are also *about* me. They are of cities and mountains and people and all the other travel-photo fodder. But my images are also about me in the sense that I have superimposed interpretation and design dynamics on the subjects. My subjects reflect my aesthetic imperatives; they become raw material to be internalized through the creative process, not something external to be captured within the confines of the viewfinder.

Photographers frequently say, "I just want a record shot." These straightforward pictures are often appreciated, and if you need one as a reminder for some personal or professional reason, by all means shoot it. But the record snapshot you took of the sunset over the cathedral too often loses all impact as the scene slides into the recesses of your memory, whereas the images into which you invest more creative energy will retain their impact. Imaginative interpretation occurs when the world is filtered through the heart and mind of a creative person striving to transcend reality and express some of the fundamental qualities of his or her own being. In the introduction to French photographer Bernard Plossu's book *New Mexico Revisited,* Hall writes, "Photographic innocence is possible, but only if the photographer aims not to capture the essence of reality but rather to create an original photographic image, in opposition to or complementing those that have come before." How to regain this photographic innocence is, of course, quite the question.

It's this childlikeness we need to recapture in our travel photography, and it has everything to do with giving ourselves unreservedly to the foreign environment and to the creative process. Because travel photography is a journey of surprise and discovery, we can allow ourselves to "regress" to our native, childlike innocence. Emboldened by the camera and freed from our daily lives at home, we can take our imaginative selves out into the world. Like a child in the sandbox of the world, we can believe anything we see; we can entertain any fantasy.

For the child, the realm of the imagination is reality. My photographic interpretations are my reality as well. And so long as I can build new photographic castles out of the sand pile of travel subject matter, I'll continue to take on the challenges of the field.

IMAGINATIVE INTERPRETATION in travel photography occurs when you remove an obvious cultural symbol from its usual setting and turn it into a personal motif. Borrowing turbans from the hotel staff of a palace hotel in India, I turned the rounds into an abstract still life reflecting my appreciation of the beauty I find in Indian ethnic dress. *(above)* Similarly, a flower vendor sold me a bouquet at a quaint café in Paris. Placed on a classic café chair, the bouquet became a symbol of charm and romance I could not resist recording. *(left)*

PARIS'S EIFFEL Tower is probably the most photographed monument in the world. "Bah, humbug!" was my longtime reaction to adding any more shots to the photo annals of the monument. However, when I spotted this painting of Notre Dame on the back side of the nearby carousel's ticket booth, I felt I had a shot at a fresh interpretation of the landmark. *(opposite)*

YOU NEED TO be just as photojournalistically alert and tactical when shooting video as you do with still travel photography. At Ocotlan, a country market outside Oaxaca, Mexico, I was just beginning to frame up these rainbow hammocks for sale when I noticed an old guy coming down the street. Calculating that he would walk in front of my video camera, I zoomed the lens to a wide angle focal length so I could capture him passing by.

WHILE DOING garbage detail is difficult when panning around the world with a video camera, I will occasionally make the effort to eliminate an unwanted element of flotsam from a scene I intend to shoot, just as I do for still shots. When I zoomed in on the man seated against the wall in back of the hammocks, I noticed the flattened cardboard box. I went in and took it out, then reshot the scene.

IN STILL photography, staying with the action and shooting a lot of film is key to capturing the single, decisive moment in the travel experience. The videographer has the advantage of being able to capture the seamless ebb and flow of local life. As I zoomed in on the hammocks, the salesman's son entered the scene and flipped the candy colored hammocks around for my benefit. Letting the camera run, I knew I had a dynamite sequence of serendipity.

THE VIDEO TRAVELER

....

VIDEOS ARE BECOMING AN INCREAS-
ingly important addition to the travel experience. While shooting in a moving
medium does differ from the taking of still images, I find that most of the creative and social issues discussed in this book are the same regardless of the
medium.

For example, understanding basic photographic issues such as composition, camera angles, and focal lengths is fundamental to shooting video. An eye
for color, graphics, texture, and light is key to any destination treatment,

whether on film or tape. The social skills required to wend one's way in various cultures as a still photographer should not be put on the back burner by the videographer. For those interested in translating a still travel-photography sensibility to the world of continuous motion and seamless visual possibility, a few points will illustrate the similarities and dissimilarities that exist in the two media.

Adjusting from the more rectilinear format of the SLR camera to the more square format of the video viewfinder and TV screen is the most pressing compositional consideration for first-time videographers. In video it may be even more important to steer clear of the point-and-shoot approach, with subjects placed smack in the middle of each frame. Since there is less chance for asymmetrical interest in square compositions, either offset the subjects stage right or stage left, or fill the frame entirely with the primary subject.

WHEN SHOOTING travel videos, I am always on the alert for footage that could establish the location or a sense of place to be used in the beginning with a title. Orange Volkswagens parked in a row against a blue wall in Oaxaca provided both an appealing image and location establishing license plates. (preceding page)

It is as important to develop dimensionality in video as it is in still imagery. The dramatic use of foreground elements can offset the potentially static square format. Organizing elements according to the rule of thirds within the frame will help, as well. Using vertical and horizontal elements, angles, and diagonals in a provocative way will also strengthen video compositions.

It's not as important in video that horizon lines be straight or buildings be absolutely vertical. In fluid situations such as real life or moving pictures, one's natural visual ballast compensates for looking up and down and all around, as it does for wild camera angles. It's actually become chic in still commercial photography, especially in the fashion industry, to deliberately skew horizon lines.

Composing in motion is like composing music: sequences should be taut and to the point. A major theme in my work is to move in as close as possible on virtually every subject. Robert Capa's comment that "if your pictures aren't strong enough, you're not close enough" applies to motion pictures and video, as well as to still photography.

As in still photography, when tracking the movement of a person in video, it is best to have the subject moving into the larger portion of the image area, regardless of whether this is from right to left or left to right. However, avoid tracking with the person right into the center of the frame.

In a pinch, if the person is moving quickly from left to right, try to keep up with him in camera right, which will exaggerate the feeling of speed. A good tracking technique is to let a person enter the image area, follow him for a while, then let him exit the image area, only to be picked up again down the street. As you track, change the focal length of the lens. If, for instance, someone is coming down the street toward the camera, zoom in while he is still far away. As he walks closer and begins to pass you, open to the wide-angle, then zoom in again as he disappears down the street. Optical variety is essential because, in editing, cuts from similar angles—for example, wide to wide—don't match up well.

Optical literacy in video is no different from still photography. The wide-angle ranges distort and spread elements across the tape or film plane. The telephoto ranges compress elements within a composition. For effective travel-video

treatments, use the entire optical range. With all the color, texture, light, and drama of the travel experience, don't just stand back with wide-angle focal lengths. Yes, shoot the overall or establishing footage in a wide-angle mode. Then remember to move in for a closer look.

Don't arrive at all your close-ups by zooming in to telephoto focal lengths. In the pursuit of overall, medium, and close-up footage, play off the camera-to-subject distance with various focal lengths. Try shooting close-ups in the wide-angle mode: dive right into the subject. As

TRANSLATING MY eye for graphic details from still to video has been the most fun aspect of shooting video travel footage. When I find a situation that conforms to my still style, I frame the subject as I would a still shot and let the camera run for a few seconds. In editing the final footage, I use these "still" frames as show stoppers.

in still photography, overall coverage of distant landscapes or city scenes might come off better at the telephoto range.

It's hard enough to control busy backgrounds even when the picture is fixed. In a moving medium, background static can be really distracting. In public places use a tight focal length when filming two people talking or engaged in business to minimize any distracting activity that would draw the viewer's eye to the rear of the image area. If you are shooting over the back of a salesperson selling oranges to a client on the far side of the produce, for example, zoom in tight on the transaction so the distant figure doesn't become obfuscated by the background hustle and bustle of the marketplace.

The use of diverse camera angles on individual subjects and situations is essential to having enough visually interesting footage for final editing. In still photography, one is apt to determine the single best camera angle on a subject and shoot it only that way. In a moving medium, it's best to capture the action coming and going. It is therefore important to develop the photojournalistic skills discussed in this book to be a fluid videographer of action.

Anticipating the development of action and moving quickly and gracefully from one place to the next are journalistic skills necessary for videographers. When taping, it's a good idea to keep the left eye open at all times so you can see people or other elements about to enter the picture area. Keeping the left eye open is also critical if you have to change positions quickly while the tape is rolling.

I FOUND USING a video camera in the Soledad Cathedral in Oaxaca, Mexico to be easier than shooting with a still camera. First of all, I was low impact from the standpoint of noise. The motor drive and shutter racket of a still camera certainly preclude being able to shoot comfortably during a silent prayer. And you can run tape satisfactorily at much lower light levels than still film.

The management of the viewer's eye is more complex in a moving medium than in stills. You manage the viewer's eye largely through your choice of camera angles. What you want people to focus on requires an optical prioritization of foreground, midground, and background elements. In a fixed, still photograph the eye has time to scan the image back and forth. The photographer has prioritized the elements in the picture, and the viewer has time to reflect on the image. With video the image is in flux—it's kinetic. Therefore, the videographer must make his or her visual priorities clear to the viewer through the skilled use of composition, camera angle, and focal length.

Videotape is cheap compared to slide or print film, so there is no excuse for not shooting lots of footage to get enough coverage of every situation you roll the video on. I find that the travel environment has more "tape-worthy" material for my video camera than I generally find "film-worthy" as a still photographer. Shooting travel stills can be a quite selective process, while shooting video demands a constant attention to the ebb and flow of local culture.

A good example of this came when I was filming a flower vendor in a Mexican market who was breast-feeding her baby. It was a long process—both activities. I got a lot of peakaction and relationship footage out of the mother and baby, but flower buyers would frequently interrupt, standing between me and the duo. So I changed camera angles to cover the business dealings, including close-ups of the flowers and other vendors; then I returned to the breast-feeding. I ended up with so much coverage of the flower market that most of it was cut. But I had shot enough footage that I had no lack of transitional imagery.

Continuity means keeping the details of location, appearance, sound, lighting, wardrobe, and props in your footage consistent from one frame or take to the next. Strict adherence to continuity is critical to videos driven by specific story lines or editorial themes. In contrast, the

WHILE IT'S BEST to use a video tripod with a fluid head to mitigate against jerky movements during panning and zooming, the image stabilization technology in most video cameras does allow for hand-holding the camera in low light with acceptable results, as I did in the Church of San Geronimo outside Oaxaca. In considering the purchase of a video camera, make sure it has the image stabilization feature.

travel experience is generally less structured: It's unpredictable and spontaneous. Although continuity can be created during editing, it is still another reason for shooting lots of tape.

A sequence of sketches plotting out a video production is called a storyboard. It outlines the beginning, middle, and end of a shooting. An obvious challenge to shooting destination videos is that the travel experience does not necessarily have a specific story line. Traveling is usually a series of unrelated experiences and unexpected encounters, and so storyboarding will not be a major concern.

Yet creating a visual thread can be a valuable exercise in travel videography. In Oaxaca, Mexico, the week before Christmas, I was shooting videotape without a specific story line or theme. Not only was I filming Christmas church services and holiday street festivities, I was also shooting the town in general as a travel experience. I needed a consistent visual device to thread through the disparate footage. It didn't take long to figure out that I could link segments together with shots of the intense color and old-world texture ubiquitous to the Mexican environment. I could then call my program "Oaxaca—The Colors of Christmas."

It is this very lack of a storyboard or structure that I most like about shooting travel videos. With visual free association I can respond to anything that strikes my aesthetic fancy. I enjoy the challenge of recognizing relationships, collecting patterns, developing themes in a foreign destination, and visualizing how they will come together in editing. A visual thread throughout a travel video can also be a stylistic one. For instance, I can try to translate my graphic-detail sensibility and eye for the idiosyncratic into a moving medium. By shooting lots of colorful close-ups I am able to maintain the integrity of my still vision on tape.

At the technical level, the two major moves for the videographer are panning and zooming. Most rookies perform both functions too fast: whether using a tripod or hand-holding the camera, slow, smooth, and easy moves are the key to successful pans and zooms.

Panning is moving the camera horizontally, right to left or left to right, in order to cover a scene that cannot be captured in a single frame. Shooting wide pans from a fixed position, either handheld or with a tripod, I find it necessary to rotate my body slightly in the direction of the pan before rolling film. This way I can complete the pan smoothly without having to adjust my footing, which can result in jiggly footage with a handheld camera or an unwanted break in the pan when using a tripod. By having your feet positioned and your body torqued in preparation for the complete pan, you eliminate the possibility of kicking the tripod. Using a fluid head on your tripod also smooths out the panning. With oil in its ball and socket, the head resists initial pressure, avoiding jerky starts and stops.

Often I make a compound move. I will zoom or vary the focal length of the lens during the take, as I am panning across a scene. With a lot of previsu-

AT OCOTLAN, a country market outside Oaxaca, I taped a sequence on a mother doing double duty selling flowers and nursing her baby. What you see here is an edited sequencing of frames as I might put them together in a finished tape. Bear in mind that these are printed single frames grabbed from the original tape. They illustrate the overall, medium, and close-up footage I shot in order to have maximum flexibility in editing the final show.

IN THE ACTUAL video show, each frame is part of footage that runs for various periods of time. Shooting from across the street, I began with wide angle footage from over the back of another vendor. My subject caught on pretty quickly that she was my prime focus of interest. Communicating with waves and giggles, it was clear she did not mind my filming her.

DURING A LULL in the action between mother and child, I zoomed in on a color intensive detail of the woman's scarf in front of me. Wanting to capture the business and confusion of the market, I let the tape roll as passersby crossed the frame, in and out of focus, and wandered the market looking for coverage of flowers and close-up abstractions of clothing or activity to create optical diversity in the final editing process.

alization and trial takes, I can select a segment of the scene I want to focus the viewer's attention on—something I might actually make a still photograph of. Then I practice the moves, positioning the zoom on the "still" shot just right and letting the camera roll a few seconds on it before opening up the zoom and panning on.

While compound moves enable me to translate my still travel-photography style into video, it's a challenge to get the precision framing that typifies my still photographs with the camera in flux. I may retake a scene several times before I feel that it has been captured.

A cut is a scene transition created in editing that instantly matches one scene with another. It is a transition that the mind and eye accept as natural. Like closing your eyes on one shot and opening them on another, the mind fills in for the nanosecond it took to make the cut.

A common mistake for first-time videographers is creating jump cuts, which occur with insufficient contrast in the focal lengths used on a sequence. In other words, you cut from a wide to a slightly less wide shot: the sequence will then appear to jump at the edit point. You need diversity of camera angles, focal lengths, and lots of coverage to maximize your editing options and produce a more professional-looking film.

The two most common special effects in video productions are the dissolve and the fade. Some video cameras actually have modes to create these effects. A dissolve entails one image fading into another and is used in film and video to create scene transitions. A dissolve also indicates the passage of time or change of location in an optically low-impact manner. For a more abrupt sense of the passage of time or location change, the fade is used. Here, the scene actually fades out completely to black or white.

Dissolves and fades can be effected either in-camera or in editing. They can, however, be overused. The more standard cut should be used most of the time for scene transitions, with the dissolve and fade introduced judiciously.

My very first video camera had a black-and-white viewfinder. But color is content in my still travel photography; without it I had nothing to hang my optical hat on. This lack of color forced me to concentrate on light and shadow, exploring how they occupied space within the square video format. I edited my first footage, shot through the monochromatic viewfinder, on a color monitor, of course, and it was quite a thrill. There was such a sense of hot and cold, of shadows and sunlight!

Video encourages acceptance of visual chaos: you get it on tape and think about it later. The often technically imperfect treatment of color and light in video, which would be unacceptable in still photographs, captures the spontaneous sense of moments and ephemera of the travel experience.

While you can add light with a battery-powered, handheld Sungun or with reflectors, it's amazing how well video comes out all by itself with low light. For instance, I was nervous about the available light for footage shot during Christmas church services in Oaxaca. I decided not to hit the "gain-up" switch, which brightens the image—gain-up is known as grain-up in the trade—and I was nonetheless very pleased with the results.

Sound is a vital part of the ephemera of the travel experience. Most video cameras record sound while you are filming, resulting in a lot of usable and unusable audio material, especially background sounds of busy streets and traffic. To create a sound track for my videos, I sometimes record "wild sound" that might be useful in editing. To do this, I turn the camera on just to record the sound; I'm not actually filming anything. Wild sound can also be captured by a separate tape recorder.

AT A RUG SHOP in Teotitlan del Valle, the famous weaving village outside Oaxaca, I was enchanted by Trabieso, a hyperactive puppy. I actually set up this situation by spreading rugs on the ground and placing the basket of bobbins on it. With the video camera on a tripod and the tape running, I induced Trabieso to perform. He tumbled into the basket, creating the best frames of the take.

But very often I am grateful for the silence of the video camera! When trying to capture spontaneous activities in markets and churches, the staccato motor drive of an SLR is often a liability. Silence is golden on tape.

Creating titles is one of the fun challenges of videography. Some camcorders incorporate a titling function and can store a title to be pulled up while filming different scenes for greater titling options. Editing systems appropriate for amateur users also include titlers. Separate titling systems provide a multitude of fonts and colors as well as create simultaneous special effects with the titles.

Titles can "travel" across the screen, zoom in or out, or scroll.

I like to collect title possibilities on location. I film the name of the place as it appears in the environment, or individual letters to spell out the destination. The letters can be cut together in editing. I also always shoot colored walls or other unbusy scenes as a background for titles.

The success of a travel video lies as much in the editing as in the actual filming. To view unedited travel tape can be deadly boring. Unless you are willing to edit your travel footage (even though it is a time-consuming process), stick to still photography.

LIKE STILL TRAVEL photographers, there is a tendency among travel videographers to just shoot wide angle, overall footage. In order to get clean close-ups of these crosses, the blue wall in the artisan's courtyard was a perfect background for them. I asked the man if I could take them out of the shop and hang them on the wall. After shooting a few seconds of overall footage, I zoomed in tighter. Incidentally, whenever I move things around, I always put them back where I found them!

If you do plan to edit your travel video into a viewable piece, conduct script supervision from the start. Make notes as to what is on each tape, subject by subject. With a microcassette recorder in my photovest, I actually note the time code for various scenes, segments, and subject matter. Having a good time-code function on the camcorder is critical to hassle-free editing. You can find what you need on various tapes quickly without having to play or shuttle through hours of tape.

Video editing requires nothing more than your camcorder, a VCR, and the cables that connect them. Simply play the videotape on the camcorder and record it on the VCR. With the VCR functions you can linear-edit the footage. While this is the simplest method, the edits are not as smooth and precise as you would get using an editing system. However, for the amateur who is just starting out on the travel-video journey, it can suffice.

I tend to feel more like a tourist with my videocamera in hand than with my still equipment, and this has considerably altered for me the social dynamics on location. As a professional travel photographer for over a quarter of a century, I have disciplined myself to move in close on people and action, incurring all the social responsibilities of this. But with a video camera I often find myself standing back and zooming in on people, rather than developing my usual optical intimacy with them. A more detached attitude can develop, justified by not wanting to alter the environment as much as I often do when shooting stills.

Because I am sometimes less assertive as a videographer in foreign environments, I am not perceived so much as a professional. I sometimes ask myself if, within the travel venue, being a videographer isn't for the creatively lazy and socially faint of heart, leaving still photography for the more dedicated interpreter of the travel experience. Is shooting travel videos akin to image-trawling of the surface experience, while working with an SLR is for the cultural and creative depth plunges?

From a more positive viewpoint, in shooting video I find I don't have to be as controlling, stopping the world to freeze-frame situations as I do for stills. With video I have learned to let the action, or continuum, flow through me. And for those venturing into travel video, I would emphasize: Make it personal. Don't just record—interpret!

As far as equipment for travel videos is concerned, I use the Canon ES5000 Hi8 camcorder, which incorporates Canon's exclusive Eye Control technology borrowed from its EOS A2E still camera. This allows you to focus the camera with your eye as you film subjects. Along with a super high-resolution color viewfinder, the ES5000 incorporates optical image stabilization technology to offset camera motion. The success of a travel video lies as much in the editing process as in the filming, and the Thumbs-Up editing system from Videonics makes this process simple and satisfying.

While there are video and film courses at many local community colleges, you might consider a workshop at a travel destination if you want to explore the medium in greater depth. For example, the Santa Fe Workshops offer film workshops for photographers. For information contact Santa Fe Workshops, P.O. Box 9916, Santa Fe, New Mexico 87504. Tel: (505) 983-1400. Also worth considering are the International Film and Television Workshops, Rockport, Maine 04856. Tel.: (207) 236-8581.

TECHNICAL CONSIDERATIONS

....

EQUIPMENT FOR THE TRAVEL PHOTOGRAPHER

From the technical standpoint, this is a confusing time for professional and amateur photographers alike. With film and camera manufacturers announcing rapid technological developments as soon as you get used to one film emulsion or camera system, something new and tempting is always on the market. I too have been confused and frustrated by these developments. Having used tried-and-true products for almost two decades, in recent years I've changed both my camera system and standard film twice!

All camera and film choices should be conscious compromises based on several criteria: aesthetic concerns, image quality, efficiency of operation, eyesight, and physical fitness. But most people begin backward when they choose their gear. They begin with what advertisers and manufacturers promise various products can do for them. Instead, you should analyze what kind of photographer you are and what kind of images you most like to make. Then ask yourself what products best enable you to accomplish your technical and aesthetic goals. If, for example, you shoot most of your photographs with a tripod, you may not need an autofocus camera system. A quick description of my own equipment choices may help to illustrate this selection process.

CAMERAS

My preference in a manual-focus camera is the Contax Rx. Not only does the lens focus with the focusing screen in the usual manner, it also has a digital focus indicator in the bottom of the viewfinder. The Contax was the first camera on the market to have autobracketing actually built into the camera body, without the need for a data back. The Contax Rx also includes a depth-of-field scale in the viewfinder. Relatively light, compact, and quiet with an elegant, discreet design and an ergonomic feel, the Contax system uses some of the sharpest lenses in the business, manufactured by Carl Zeiss.

Because I now need reading glasses, I recently decided to investigate autofocus camera systems. The Canon EOS-1N, with its superfast, silent UltraSonic lenses, became my choice. The control dial on the back of the camera is the easiest way

ON A WALK in Wales I made a still life illustration of my experience by collecting feathers, thistles, and flowers along the trail. I arranged them in a pocket of my photovest, which was lying on a stone wall, and took a photograph with a 60mm macro lens. I often illustrate my travel experience with personal pictures of this sort. *(page 176)*

to change modes. More important, with the ability to customize autofocus and metering in different zones in the viewfinder, I finally feel free of the compositional tyranny of center-biased autofocus systems.

I use an architectural grid in my cameras. Used by many professional architectural photographers, this faintly etched Bauhaus grid of squares is a great aid in composing photographs, in keeping horizon lines straight, and buildings plumb and square. The grid does not interfere with normal viewing and makes organizing the different elements in the viewfinder so much easier.

If your camera system does not include a grid screen, you can have one custom-etched by a professional camera-repair shop. The only possible drawback of the architectural screen is that it can become a crutch if you begin to force all your compositions into conformity with the grid.

BAGS, VESTS, AND STRAPS

For carrying my cameras, I use the two-and-a-half-inch-wide Op/Tech Pro Camera Strap, made of stretchy neoprene. It allows the cameras to bounce a bit as I walk and makes them seem much lighter. I recently changed my traditional camera bag for a Lowepro Mini-Treker backpack-style camera bag. With all the weight no longer on one shoulder, this has relieved me of neck and shoulder strain. The backpack can also be carried with a shoulder strap or top handle, which is useful when I might be in danger of pickpocketing attempts, or when I need quick access to the gear.

I also wear photovests. These are ideal for keeping unexposed film at the ready and for quick stashing of exposed rolls. I have a variety of vests—long, short, color coordinated—and switch between them depending on assignment, travel, or sartorial needs. While wearing the backpack over the photovest, I stash such accessories as filters, lip gloss, money, and minirecorder into all the pockets. I don't mind that a photovest makes me more conspicuous as a photographer; I've never found it did me any good to be secretive about my photographic intentions.

TRIPODS

Most tripods are either overkill or underkill for a standard 35mm camera. A tripod that is too big is a literal drag; a wimpy tripod is close to useless. People with perfectly good tripods often fail to screw the camera properly on the head or make sure the handles and legs are stable. I see people extending tripod legs so that the weight of the camera is not distributed evenly among them, and on uneven terrain, they don't make sure the center of gravity of their cameras falls straight to the ground.

But a good tripod well used is a great addition to travel photography. I use a tripod for 75 percent of my pictures. Because I'm not after the point-and-shoot grab shot as much as I used to be, I enjoy setting up a camera on a tripod. Currently I use the Gitzo Mountaineer

carbon fiber tripod with the Joystick Bogen head. It is a light and simple combination.

The tripod enables me to make adjustments in the subject before I shoot; I can walk away from the camera, move something, and return to the camera knowing my composition will not be sacrificed. With a tripod and automatic bracketing on my camera, I can stand up and use a cable release to make incredibly fast exposures. Onlookers don't even know I've taken the picture.

This technique can save your neck and back from the strain of being in an awkward semi-upright position and always having to look through the viewfinder. If you become handy with a good tripod, it won't slow you down much. While it may be a drag to lug the thing around all day, it saves the energy of hand-holding shots.

Many solid tripods are too bulky, cumbersome, and awkward for travel photography. When shopping for a tripod, try to get as much strength and extension in as small a package as possible. I like tripods that can go low to the ground for nature shots or for extreme angles on architecture. Stay clear of tricky tripods with plastic release tabs that can snap off and extension handles that can get bent. I prefer ball-head mounts for the camera over the panhead type. Quick releases are also useful. Make sure you get one that really battens down the camera and doesn't allow it to slide onto the ground.

FLASH

On professional assignments, I'll frequently use up to seven strobe units on an interior shot of a hotel or restaurant. But for general travel photography, I don't like using single flash units, mainly because I don't want to carry the flash around. I'd rather use a tripod and get more natural-light effects. In the past the unskilled use of single-source flash units resulted in photos with harsh shadows and unnatural effects. Today this problem has been rectified by the "smart flash," such as the Metz 40 MZ-2.

With a tilt-head flash unit or connecting cord, it is also possible to use the technique of bounce flash. Obviously, this only works when there is a white or reflective surface, a wall or low ceiling, near your subject.

I'm not a fan of bounce cards, mini-umbrellas and diffusion balloons attached to a flash unit. I don't want to look like a Rube Goldberg contraption, and in any case, these gadgets are awkward to maneuver in a vertical-format shot.

FLIPPING LIGHT

For additional light, I slip a Fotoflex LiteDisc into the inside zipper pocket of my photovest. Available in various sizes, the reflector curls into a small diameter and unfurls into a larger disc that is either silver or gold on one side, white on the other. The silver produces a cooler light, the gold a warmer. With the general warmth of ISO 100 slide films these days, I use the silver. If I need additional warmth, I pop on an 81A warming filter.

I use the disc to bounce light into shadowy areas of a composition or to kick light into a face for a portrait shot. It takes a second party to pull this off, unless you have the camera on a tripod and a long cable release so you can position yourself away from the camera to work the disc. If the camera is set up in a shadow area, you may need a twenty-foot cable release so you can get into the sun with the LiteDisc.

FILTERS

I use filters sparingly. The signature color saturation in my work comes from underexposing slide film, rather than from filter use. If you do use filters, you should be willing to undertake a lot of trial and error. Filter use does not guarantee a better picture, and they can in fact become a crutch in your photography. I've never been fond of soft focus, star, multiple-image, dream, or color-prism effects. For some photographers, however, experimenting with these filters is fun, although orchestrating them properly requires talent, experience, and artistic judgment.

I do use amber-colored 81A and 81B warming filters to add warmth to a scene on a flat day or for a warmer interpretation of a subject. I also have UV filters on each of my lenses to protect them from the elements and to cut down on the bluish, cooling effects of ultraviolet light. If you shoot prints, you could use skylight filters that have a pinkish cast to warm up color negative film.

Be sure you only have one filter on the lens at a time. Extending the lens barrel by stacking up filters will cause vignetting or dark corners on your photographs.

MOTOR DRIVES

Motor drives are essential to my travel photography. Most SLR cameras today have either motor drives or autowinders built into the camera body. I use my motor drives to capture sequential images of activities in marketplaces and at festivals or special events. I also find that a motor drive enables me to hand-hold the camera steady at slower shutter speeds. Not having to manually advance the film, which always jiggles the camera, I can maintain a precise composition and make several motor-driven exposures.

FILM

Regardless of where you go, film will almost always be cheaper to buy in the United States than abroad. If you don't use it all, stick the unexposed rolls in the refrigerator when you get home. This way it will stay fresh until you are ready to use it. Be sure to read the expiration date on the film boxes, though.

Many amateurs prefer color negative or print films because prints are easier to show around. However, print films are more vulnerable to the vicissitudes of processing than are slide films. While setting up the projector for slide shows can be tiresome, shooting slide film is cheaper in the long run, and you can always have standard prints made from your favorite

slides at a good custom lab.

Professional film emulsions are aged to the point of peak color balance and are then refrigerated by the manufacturer. They are delivered to the camera stores in this condition, where they are again popped into a refrigerator. When a pro buys professional emulsions, he or she shoots them immediately and has them processed shortly thereafter.

Amateur emulsions of film, on the other hand, are sent to the stores before they've aged to optimum color balance. It is expected that the film will sit on the dealer's shelf for a while, and then it might sit in the camera to age for months between babies or holidays. Although pro film must be used quickly, you might decide that the improved quality is worth the extra cost.

PUSHING FILM

When caught without high-speed film, I will "push" my usual ISO 100 film one or two stops. To achieve this, I set my ISO speed for double the actual rating of the film. For example, I will rate ISO 100 film at ISO 200 for a one-stop push or at ISO 400 for a two-stop push. This adjustment of the ISO rating fools the camera's light meter. However, you must remember to tell your photo finisher that you have pushed the film. Otherwise it will be processed normally and all your pictures will come out too dark, or not at all. Also, once you have adjusted the ISO dial on the camera, you must shoot the entire roll at that rating.

PHOTO STORAGE AND CD-ROM

My slide storage system is as simple as it gets. I keep slides in 20th Century Plastics sheets that hold twenty 35mm transparencies. And these sheets are simply filed according to destination in standard filing cabinets.

Eventually, I'll get around to a more sophisticated archiving of my favorite images. For this purpose, Kodak's Photo CD system is ideal. You can create photo CD albums of vacation photos from either 35mm slides or negatives. Photo CDs allow you to show friends your vacation photos on your TV or personal computer, using a CD-interactive unit or a photo CD player. With a Photo CD Custom Imaging Kit or Kodak's Portfolio software, you can create your own electronic travel album.

For a custom production of CD-ROM slide shows, and for electronic photo restoration and color balancing of faded slides, you may wish to contact a service bureau such as:

Steven Miller, Miller Imaging
2718 Wilshire Boulevard
Santa Monica, CA 90403
(310) 264-4711

Kim Kapin, ZZYZX
949 North Highland Avenue
Los Angeles, CA 90038
(800) 995-1025

WHAT TO BRING AND HOW TO PACK

For assignment travel photography, I take two Canon camera bodies, the EOS-1N and the A2E. I keep a 20–35mm wide-angle lens on one body and a 100mm macro or 80–200mm zoom on the other. In addition, I take my 35–350mm superzoom lens for landscapes or for special events that require constant zooming in and out. While I generally use a tripod with the superzoom, I find it to be hand-holdable, as well.

The equipment requirements change when I'm out shooting for myself. The camera backpack and second camera stay in the hotel room. So does the superzoom. On goes the photovest. The lens I use most, the 100mm macro, goes on the EOS-IN, and the 20–35mm zoom goes in a vest pocket, along with enough film for the day, usually ten to fifteen rolls. Sometimes the 80–200mm rides in a Lowepro fanny pack face forward for easy access. An 81A warming filter, a small Fotoflex Lite-Disc reflector, a cable release, a few lengths of electrical tape, and a Swiss Army knife are the only extras. Depending on my stamina at the time, sometimes the tripod gets lugged along.

ON FOOT

The photovest is indispensable on adventure trips. While trekking in Nepal, I carried one camera body with the 20–35mm zoom attached; I had two additional lenses—the 100mm macro and the 80–200mm zoom—stuffed into the vest's pouches, plus a tele-extender just in case. A backup camera was in my duffel.

I carried a camera around my waist on a wide, heavy-duty Op/Tech Pro strap. I customized the strap by cutting it and splicing it together with electrical tape so it fitted around my lower back, with the camera body hanging in a marsupial fashion on my stomach. The quick release on the strap enabled me to whisk the camera from my waist for fast responses to photographic possibilities. When sweat stretched out the strap too much, I simply took in another bit with my Swiss Army knife and tape.

On treks with camera gear, I've found that I'm happier with the camera on my stomach rather than hanging around my neck and strapped to my chest with one of those fancy straps. With both a photovest and a backpack occupying my upper torso, I want to distribute the rest of my gear around my body. A couple days of field-testing my system proved my calculations right, for me!

On an Outward Bound wilderness-skills program in Utah, I took the Olympus Infinity Superzoom camera. With its fully automatic metering and focusing features and its 35–120mm zoom lens, this lightweight "bridge" camera was the ideal solution for getting a good range of pictures without carrying a full-fledged SLR with interchangeable lenses. The small camera rode in a fanny pack swung around to the front.

ON SAFARI

I've learned to customize my gear according to the particular adventure. For example, on African safaris, if you know you're going to be shooting from a van with other photographers, don't do what I did the first time, which was to take a standard tripod, thinking I could extend it from the van floor. You can't spread out the legs of a tripod with four or five other shooters in a van, and using it mono-pod fashion is much too unstable. Next time, either I'll take a beanbag that I'll place on the roof of the van as a camera cushion, or I'll plant a tabletop tripod on the back or front roof, with a monoball head for quick adjustments. I'll also be sure my tripod feet have rubber tips so I don't get my driver angry because I've scratched his roof.

If I go to Africa again, I would also take the Canon 35–350mm UltraSonic zoom lens. Given how close one gets to wildlife on safari, this lens would enable me to capture all shots without any lens changes. With a long-range telephoto lens on safari, I used a fast, flexible slide film. Going on low-light dawn and dusk game runs, I used an ISO 400 film that could be "pushed" as far as ISO 1600. I liked the grainy effects I got from pushing the film; it gave me the textural interpretation I wanted of the safari experience.

ON HORSEBACK

On horseback trips in the American West, I wear a photovest. While in the saddle, I limit myself to three lenses: a wide-angle, and medium and telephoto zooms. Extra lenses either ride in the photovest or get wrapped in chamois cloths and stashed in the saddlebags. As on treks, I pack a second camera body and other lenses in my duffel.

Not wanting a camera body clanging around my neck along the trail, I hung it from the saddle horn, using the leather thongs on the saddle that normally secure a cowboy's rope. I wrapped the camera in a Domke bag to protect the body from saddle sores. With the bag's Velcro closures, it was easy to grab the camera for quick shots from the saddle. A decent camera should be able to handle a ride like this; however, I have a "wear and tear" body that can take rougher treatment.

Many systems and solutions are on the market for coping with gear on adventure trips. *Outdoor Photographer* magazine is an excellent source for these products. While I find many of them tempting, I usually end up trusting my own ingenuity and customizing my packing systems according to the individual demands of the experience.

CHECKLIST FOR TRAVEL PHOTOGRAPHERS

If I tried to fit all the items listed below into my camera bag, I'd be grounded. The accessories you take will be a personal compromise based on past needs and uses. Each item deserves consideration, however, and I include many of them in either my bag or photovest. I take some things on a trip just in case of an emergency.

- Large, heavy-duty Ziploc plastic bags for protecting cameras from rain, salt water, or dust. I also use them for both unexposed and exposed film.
- A compact electronic flash with an extension-coil cord.
- A cable release for time-exposure and motor-driven sequences.
- Denatured alcohol and a soft cloth or cotton swabs for cleaning cameras and lenses.
- Dust Off in the small travel size for blasting dust and other debris from camera gear.
- A small soft brush for getting into the tight spots on camera gear.
- Liquid lens cleaner and lens tissue.
- A set of jeweler's screwdrivers to tighten the small screws that can jiggle loose from vibrations caused by car or plane travel.
- A Swiss Army knife with multiple tools. This is essential.
- A small pocket flashlight with fresh batteries for reading the camera controls and readouts during night photography.
- Business cards, model releases if needed, a spiral notebook, pens. Also a compact cassette recorder for quick on-location fact-taking.
- Passport. Always have it with you.
- The tripod of your choice or an alternative camera support.
- Spare lens caps for the fronts and backs of all your lenses, in case you lose one.

- Lens shades for every lens in your bag. These prevent lens flare with backlighting and strong sidelighting; each lens should have its own shade so you don't have to switch them.
- A plastic rain bonnet that folds to the size of a packet of tissues, or a shower cap, to cover your camera and lens in an unexpected downpour.
- A large flat rubber disc (sold as a kitchen-sink stopper), or a lighter piece cut from a rubber glove, to unscrew stuck filters or lens shades.
- A small canvas filter wallet to consolidate all your filters so you don't have to unscrew each filter from its plastic case every time you need one.
- Instruction manuals for cameras and flash units.
- Compass for figuring out the direction of sunrise and sunset.
- Tissues, dark glasses, sunscreen, and any other personal items you need.

THE ETHICS OF TIPPING

When it comes to tipping in travel photography, I try to keep it light—and keep it in my pocket. With mass tourism permeating practically every niche and cranny of the earth, being asked for *something* in exchange for a photograph is an ever-increasing occurrence. Every travel photographer of conscience must consider the ethics of tipping and how to react to requests for money, candy, pens, or Polaroids. What justifies either proffering these items or withholding them? People have strong feelings and opinions; I certainly have mine. In sharing my experiences and opinions based on over thirty years of worldwide travel photography, I certainly do not expect everyone to agree with me.

In general, I have found that travelers are all too willing to tip in exchange for photographs of people, and even for pictures of buildings or produce in an open-air market. While this may seem like a harmless gesture of goodwill that greases the photographic wheel, many photographers have not really considered the impact of tipping.

The effects of tourism and the impact of Western culture on "paradise" are explored in a fascinating book by Pico Iyer. The young Anglo-Indian author traveled throughout Asia to observe the hybridization of authentic cultures with Western influences. In *Video Night in Kathmandu* (Knopf), Iyer writes, "If the First World is not invariably corrupting the Third, we are sometimes apt to leap to the opposite conclusion: that the Third World, in fact, is hustling the First. As tourists, moreover, we are bombarded with importunities from such a variety of locals—girls who live off their bodies and louts who live off their wits, merchants who use friendship to lure us into their stores and 'students' who attach themselves to us in order to improve their English—that we begin to regard ourselves as beleaguered innocents and those we meet as shameless predators."

Iyer's observations convey how unpleasant the travel experience can at times be. And for the travel photographer, the issue of tipping for pictures must be added to his litany of foreign frustrations. But should all these hassles go away just to make the tourist experience more pleasant? Why shouldn't people under touristic siege take every possible advantage of the marauding masses? As Iyer notes, "We are there by choice and they largely by circumstance . . . that we are traveling in the spirit of pleasure, adventure, and romance, while they are mired in the more urgent business of trying to survive . . . they must stake their hopes on every potential transaction."

A travel photographer is automatically perceived as a "potential transaction." But this is no excuse for capitulating to every request for a tip just because we really want a picture. Although this may sound hard-hearted, as if I'm trying to keep the world poor by not allowing myself to be hustled, I believe it is simply realistic: my spare change is not going to improve anyone's lot.

I disapprove of tipping for pictures because I value my experiences with people too much. I go to great lengths to establish a rapport with my subjects in order get the caliber of portrait I want. The onus is on me to make sure the photographic encounter is a pleasant one for them. My subjects have accepted me as an individual: they don't label me as a tourist, neither do I label them as poor.

Past experience has taught me that when I have paid for people pictures, I have gotten a business deal, not a personal exchange. I get a snap a buck. And buying poses does nothing toward establishing rapport with people who live in different cultures. I don't find passing out Polaroids to be a useful solution, either. What are you supposed to do when thirty children in a village all want a Polaroid? Cut the print in thirty pieces? Or take thirty shots? Occasionally, however, a subject will ask me to send them a print of the picture I took of them. This request I do believe in honoring. Despite the considerable cost in printing and mailing, I make sure to send prints.

Whenever someone asks me for a tip, there's always a moment of discomfort. I have the option of graciously ducking out of the deal. But over the years, I've learned to treat these encounters like a game, a test of my wit. Many times I've discovered that the other person considers it a game too. If they can extract a buck from me, fine; if not, well, they were just testing me. It's a friendly sport, never taken too personally by either side.

If it is a game, then how you play it is all-important. Intuition, spontaneity, and humor are my guides in how to handle each encounter. Staying loose and not overreacting have often enabled me to finesse financial demands and clear the way for photography. Recently I've tried to adopt a more relaxed, philosophical, unacquisitive attitude about people photography in general. To the degree that I no longer want to charm or coerce people into being my subjects, I also have no problem forgoing a shot if it's clearly a "tip 'em or lose 'em" situation. Demanding a tip is some people's polite way of asking me to leave. It does no one a service to take these cross-cultural dynamics personally.

Above all, I refuse to turn locals into "services rendered." I do not view the world's people as consumer goods, as commodities who *should* pose for photographs to ensure I have good vacation pictures. Nor are they characters from central casting with a per-snap price. This is especially true with young people. In many countries, children ask for balloons, candy, or pens—they're not seeking survival change. While it may seem harmless to pass out these items, I find the "gimme game" dehumanizing, treating children like cute inhabitants of the world's zoo waiting for tossed goodies like so many peanuts.

I believe the motivations for tipping all boil down to three: guilt, laziness, and insecurity. Guilt manifests itself in the emotional blackmail of "I'm rich and they're poor." Laziness claims it's just so much easier to tip. Insecurity causes you to reach for your wallet out of cultural disorientation and personal uncertainty. After analyzing these sentiments, I've come to my personal ethic of tipping. Which is not to do it.

OUTSMARTING AIRPORT X RAYS

There's no denying that to put your gear and film through airport clearance checks is fraught with uncertainty, despite airport attempts to allay these concerns. The potential effects of x-raying film depend on three factors: the ASA rating or light sensitivity of the film, the strength of the X ray, and the number of times the film has been exposed. It has been demonstrated that airport X-raying has a cumulative effect on film. In practical terms, this means that slow-speed color films, such as ISO 25, 50, or 64 daylight film, can be passed through a normal X-ray machine in most airports quite a few times without danger. Problems arise when you are traveling through several countries with variously adjusted X-ray machines and various speeds of film. Because high-speed films are more vulnerable to X-ray exposure, many airports post a sign to remove these films from carry-on bags going through the X-ray machine.

I always include at least five rolls of some high-speed film as a ploy to get a hand check of the special case I transport my film in. I use one of those movie-film-type cases with cross straps and a handle, which I've lined with heavy-duty Filmshield bags. You can also buy special plastic boxes that have a lead inner lining.

My guerrilla warfare X-ray checkpoint tactics consist of taking the lid off the film box before reaching the inspector. I announce that some rolls of high-speed emulsion film are somewhere in the box, which often has up to 150 rolls of film in clear canisters, all neatly lined up. The attendant can easily see what's in each clear canister: I make it so easy for them that they can hardly refuse the hand check. With this technique, I've managed to get hand checks in European airports notorious for their indifference to photographers. If I do have to cave in and send the box through the X-ray machine, I just pray the machine isn't set too high.

Other photographers take all of their film out of the boxes and plastic canisters and place them in a clear Ziploc bag. I think this is fine except I don't like breaking the vacuum seal on the canisters before I actually shoot film. If your preferred film comes in opaque canisters, you may want to crack them, since a plastic bag full of black canisters usually does not satisfy an inspector's curiosity.

In addition, be prepared with your film well in advance of reaching the X-ray checkpoint. Avoid being in a flap and dropping your stuff around. Be courteous and patient. Incidentally, it's a calculated risk to arrive early for your flight in hopes of getting a less harried inspector. The inspector with time on his hands can give you more problems than the one who needs to push you through quickly at the last minute.

X rays won't have a detrimental effect on videotape or audiotape. But the strong magnetic field in the walk-through metal detectors can cause problems with these materials. If you can, ask for a hand inspection here too.

Some airports also x-ray checked luggage; others only spot-check suitcases. When it occurs, high dosages are used, which may blow right through heavy Filmshield bags. Therefore, packing film in checked luggage is a risk. I ask the airline check-in attendant if checked luggage gets hit at either end of the flight before I feel safe sending it through. But then, even with the attendant's assurances, who really knows for sure?

INDEX